SHAKESPEARE'S CULTURE OF VIOLENCE

Shakespeare's
Culture of Violence

DEREK COHEN
Associate Professor of English
York University, Ontario, Canada

St. Martin's Press

First published in Great Britain 1993 by
THE MACMILLAN PRESS LTD
Houndmills, Basingstoke, Hampshire RG21 2XS
and London
Companies and representatives
throughout the world

A catalogue record for this book is available
from the British Library.

ISBN 0–333–57088–X

Printed in Great Britain by
Ipswich Book Co Ltd
Ipswich, Suffolk

First published in the United States of America 1993 by
Scholarly and Reference Division,
ST. MARTIN'S PRESS, INC.,
175 Fifth Avenue,
New York, N.Y. 10010

ISBN 0–312–07258–9

Library of Congress Cataloging-in-Publication Data
Cohen, Derek.
Shakespeare's culture of violence / Derek Cohen.
    p.   cm.
Includes bibliographical references and index.
ISBN 0–312–07258–9
1. Shakespeare, William, 1565–1616—Political and social views.
2. Shakespeare, William, 1564–1616—Histories.   3. Literature and
society—England—History—16th century.   4. Violence in literature.
I. Title.
PR3024.C6   1993
822.3'3—dc20   91–31845
                                                             CIP

To my beloved children, Sam and Sophie

Contents

Acknowledgements

Chapter 2 appeared in a different form in the *Shakespeare Survey* (1985) and Chapter 3 in *Shakespeare Studies* (XXI). I should like to acknowledge the receipt of a grant from York University's Faculty of Arts. For her support and generosity I most gratefully thank Sheila Barry. I would also like to acknowledge the friendship of Lois Woolf, Hazel Cohen, Bob Casto, Jan de Crespigny, Kenneth Gibson, Magnus Gunther, Deborah Heller, David Shugarman, and Don Summerhayes. For their hospitality and old, deep friendship I thank Cobber and Joan Smith.

1
Introduction

This book is a study of the cultural and political manifestations of violence in eight Shakespeare plays. It attempts to explore both the deliberate and the spontaneous uses to which violence is put in public and personal life and to understand the ways in which violence, however passionately it is used, is always a cultural sign, part of an inescapably complex system of codes of expression. Acts of violence belong to patriarchy as surely as fathers do. They appear in these plays to issue directly from that system, indeed, are often logical, rational products of it. I am proposing that within the plays there are no random acts of violence, that even where the violent act seems most sudden and unplanned, it can be demonstrated to function as an inherent feature of the political system of patriarchal authority. Thus, though violence is constructed in the established laws and codes as anti-social, though the violent act is punishable by law and called cruel and unnatural, it is the very system that so condemns it that produces it and, occasionally, needs and depends on it. And so it must, for that system acquires integrity from its representation as 'natural' of an ideology of suppression and resistance. It is the problem of patriarchy to suppress the resistance that suppression creates. It can, in short, never put an end to that resistance because its existence depends upon that suppression.

Violence, both criminal and legitimate, is an essential form of cultural expression though it is always the dominant culture within society which gets to define criminality and legitimacy. For this reason acts of violence are all political in that they are absorbed by and conform to and, additionally, are produced by a social code which valorizes order as a social value. In patriarchal societies that order is achieved by the rigourous maintenance of class divisions and sustained by the political determination that all illegitimate violence is harmful to all classes. Simultaneously, that same politics has ensured that violent crime is a fact of life for the poor and weak in overwhelmingly larger measure than it is for the rich and powerful. Violent crime is horrifying partly because immanent to it is the threat of revolution, of disregard for social order. Just as the poor derive least benefit from the wealth of society, so the social order is constructed to imply that they who have most to gain from change shall lose most by violent revolution. While the rich may lose much, the poor may lose everything. Within capitalist societies the poor are kept on this side of desperation through various kinds of welfare and social opportunity. The effect of this – conveniently for the ruling class – is to provide them with something to lose by revolution, that minimal stability and security which they have a stake in preserving and which is seen as preferable to the upheaval of revolution.

Where Shakespeare's plays stand in relation to the issues of violence, legitimacy, and illegitimacy is largely a textual question. The following chapters attempt to address the related question of whether Shakespeare's texts are complicitous with the process of control that they dramatize. The issue of whether or not the plays are exposing or simply complying with patriarchal structures underlies these, and possibly all, readings of Shakespeare. To recognize their ambiguity is to take one step away from the intentionalist argument that Shakespeare's own voice can be heard amongst the thousands of voices of his characters, a position that implies the presence within the plays of an ultimate authority to which all questions may be referable. But even to recognize ambiguity is to propose the existence of a clever author and central authority who has, in a sense, outsmarted those readers who have missed that ambiguity. The text is an infinitely mutable and tractable thing; it is as variable as its readers are different. To the question, then, of whether the texts are complicitous with or revealing of patriarchal forms, one answer is that they do indeed expose patriarchy, often while seeming to proclaim it. The following arguments derive from the belief that the most rewarding and productive reading starts from the position of disbelief, of refusing to take on faith and at face value the words on the page. This is not to discredit the author, but rather to allow for the widest range of displacements and deferrals of potential meaning that the text is capable of producing, confident in the knowledge that these are infinite because the text cannot exist in some pristine form but is always mediated. Distrust of authority – even or especially that of the author – is both a theme and a nervous presence in the plays themselves; it must be the reader's constant guide.

The second tetralogy is examined as a group of plays in which a politics of violence is explored and developed. From *Richard II* where monarchy loses its grip on the instruments of control and suppression, the plays represent a movement through difficulty and uncertainty to, in *Henry V*, a moment in Shakespeare's history where violence is finally harnessed by the patriarchal authority and used successfully to consolidate monarchy. The tragedies, *Titus Andronicus*, *King Lear*, and *Othello*, are a means of pursuing the same notion on a more domestic scale. They are the only plays by Shakespeare in which female protagonists are murdered by men; they seem, therefore, peculiarly apposite subjects in an exploration of relations of power and violence within patriarchy. Lavinia, Cordelia, and Desdemona provide the focus for an analysis of patriarchy as represented and experienced by its subject members. Though this matter is partially examined in studying the histories, the fact that the subjects here are all women gives a particular gender-based perspective to the analysis. The gender difference is all-important and is linked directly to the mode and reason for the violent deaths of these female characters. *Macbeth* epitomizes these issues of difference and authority. It provides a vivid instance of difference itself under threat. Its violence encompasses and redefines the categories upon which patriarchy stands: and violence almost succeeds in collapsing difference in upon itself. In posing the threat and then lifting it the play only appears to come out in favour of patriarchal order whose tentativeness, fragility, and vulnerability have been dangerously exposed.

Patriarchal authority is the authority invested in individual men who are represented by that authority as being able and obliged to pass on their power, voluntarily or not, to other individual men. Part of the reason only men enjoy patriarchal authority is, simply, that they are men – that is, a kind of 'natural' or biological basis determines that selection. Patriarchal authority, by definition an exclusive authority, belongs to that form of political practice which nurtures individualistic endeavour at the expense of the collectivity. Its highest goals – exemplified by its gods and monarchs – include the accretion of all power into the sphere of a single man: realistically, of course, this ideal translates itself into the concentration of different degrees of power into the hands of many individual men (and, occasionally, women), including, in our cultural terms, kings, princes, nobles, magistrates, generals, ensigns, fathers, sons, brothers. While the list could go on, it *is* finite and as ideologically revealing in what it omits as in what it includes. There is a counter-vocabulary, a lexis of non-authority and submission which embraces the subjects of the patriarchal order. That lexis includes and encompasses women, children, the serving class and the poor. Part of the role of ideology in socializing these subjects is to teach them not to desire power. It – the dominant ideology – often represents women as duplicitous and disruptive.[1] The contradiction between the belittling of women and the simultaneous representation of them as threatening to patriarchy is one of the more palpable indices of the justifiably paranoic nature of the patriarchal system which depends upon the discursive forces of ideology for its own defence.

Between these two groups – the one of men only, the other of powerless men, children and women – there exists, almost by definition, a state of conflict. The men with power wish to keep their power, those without power desire power, are indeed taught by the value structure of patriarchy to desire power, notwithstanding the contradictory attempts that patriarchy makes to teach the powerless not to desire power. That which is worth having is that which others have. Thus a state of subversion and resistance seems natural and inevitable. An unequal power structure, contingent as it is upon social and political imbalance, must produce turbulence as the power axis shifts and is shifted by desire and possibility. Ultimately, of course, access to power may be through violence, which is itself an ideologically determined practice, conforming to the various kinds of ideology identified by Raymond Williams. He notes that ideology – and hence those formations that come under its heading – can be used to describe both the *'formal and conscious beliefs* of a class . . . or the less conscious, less formulated attitudes, habits and feelings, or even unconscious assumptions, bearings and commitments'.[2] Or, indeed, both forms simultaneously. Shakespeare's political plays and his tragedies demonstrate what Williams recognizes as the artificiality of the difference. The political plays identify the formally dominant ideologies of monarchy and patriarchy and their protagonists expend themselves in attempting to sustain what is consciously constructed as the political and personal interest of those in power. The action of the tragedies, engaged, as it always is, with the relation of the subject to the dominant ideology, refocuses the tenets of the ruling class onto a struggle between the single subject and the formal modes and notions of power. The effect is to expose the ways in which that formal ideological practice is self-sustaining and contradictory. It is for this reason that materialist analysis tends to avoid the term 'individual' in favour of 'subject': 'individual' implies a highly improbable kind of indivisibility of the 'subject', who always is, as Jonathan Dollimore argues, informed instead precisely by those contradictory and ideological processes which the dramas uncover.[3] The concept and presence of class differentiation is the chief means by which the ruling elites serve their own interests. Related to this is the question of the deployment of women into different classes, a practice which helps to naturalize the class structure and to develop and sustain division amongst women who, though in one sense an oppressed group with the common interest of an oppressed group, are simultaneously separated from each other by the class system. It is a constant subject of contemporary political debate. As Peter Stallybrass puts it, 'Oppressed groups . . . by denying the class differentiation of women, may attack aristocratic privilege. But when the elimination of class boundaries is produced by the collapsing of women into a single undifferentiated group, that elimination is commonly articulated within misogynistic discourse.'[4] The sixteenth century produced a single but vital exception to the rule of men, and seems to have been preoccupied with the procrustean task of naturalizing the anomalous monarchy of Elizabeth. However, Leonard Tennenhouse asserts that the Elizabethans saw the state as no less patriarchal for being embodied as a female, 'and they saw the queen as no less female for possessing patriarchal powers. In other words, the idea of a female patriarch appears to have posed no contradiction in terms of Elizabethan culture.'[5]

The plays studied in this book all provide instances of the use and the usurpation of power and the relation of class and gender differentiation to power. Yet, of course, they do so in very different ways. The history plays are overtly political and demonstrate the conduct of men within the wavering confines of monarchy. The pale of authority widens to accommodate new conditions and terms. In *Richard II* the monarch tries vainly to hold onto his authority. It is when he fails that we get an idea of the absolute hold of patriarchy over the political system and the monarch himself. His greatest obligation is to his monarchy, to the patriarchal structure which maintains him. The fall of Richard II comes about because Richard disobeys the rules that govern the governor. His own weakness is not as important as his willingness to weaken the system: that is the betrayal for which he pays with his life. Richard is replaced by a monarch who simply wants Richard's power for himself. His ascent to the throne is accomplished by the support he gets from the alienated nobility; this is a fact sometimes lost because of the play's determined concentration on the two individuals in contention for the throne. There is fairly frequent mention in the drama of the poor and the disenfranchized citizens cheering Bolingbroke on his way to greatness, but the visible omission of these people of whom we only hear says a good deal about their importance as enablers of the system. In effect they have no impact on the change of leaders in the play. Their physical absence is a significant gap in the narrative. Why are they mentioned at all, these draymen who bid Bolingbroke Godspeed on his way to exile, as if in direct defiance of Richard's rule? Their greeting to an enemy of the king is only one of many signs of the discontented and subversive energy among the poor in the histories.

In *Henry IV* 1 and 2, Bolingbroke's son, the heir apparent, is seen studying the ways of monarchy and power. And, of course, he is a ready learner. In Part 1 he embraces violence as his instrument of rule and conquest through a series of actions which teach him the value of violence as a political tool. In committing himself to violent ways, Hal virtually consecrates the violent method through a ritualized oath-taking that fastens him to the patriarchal monarchy he has long avoided. In vowing to kill Hotspur, Hal is deliberately choosing duality as a political instrument. There are for him two levels of action, one of patriarchally and socially sanctioned violence, the other of poverty, anarchy, and criminal violence. He learns that the difference is artificial, is determined ideologically and is contingent on power. Every critic accepts that the king is as corrupt at least as Falstaff, yet it is habitual to praise Hal for choosing the king's power over Falstaff's because, presumably, critics like most people prefer what they call 'responsible government'. What this play, and Part 2, and *Henry V* demonstrate with great vividness is that the patriarchal power structures are so embedded in the known cultural and political forms from which the plays issue that its only acknowledged alternative is a politics of poverty so violent and anarchic as to terrify any sane citizen. We have been taught to applaud the banishment of Falstaff at the end of part 2 because he presides over a world of lawlessness, violence, and killing and advocates lawlessness as a tool of social control. In doing so we fall into the trap of taking a lesson from the text, of seeing it as complicitous with our and its dominating cultural values. We need to remain aware, however, that Falstaff's world is a product, perhaps a deliberate product, of the culture and politics of the Henrys; *their* lawlessness, violence, and killing are roughly crammed into the confines of the legitimacy which they determine. The text quietly insists that poverty and its concomitants of crime and rage emerge directly out of the patriarchy of this culture over which Henry reigns. Whether Hal knows this must be forever uncertain. However, his embrace of duality is a tacit and deeply ambivalent decision to perpetuate the process and maintain the values of the patriarchal structure; in short, to keep order by keeping the power hierarchy essentially the same. Changes, of course, will occur under his reign, but these will be shifts within predictable determined boundaries.

The most dramatic change occurs when Hal becomes king. Between Richard and Bolingbroke there is little to choose. But King Hal introduces sweeping differences with his reign. Primarily, of course, he possesses the one thing Richard and his father most desire, the loyalty of his nobles. Of the exceptions – Scroop, Grey, and Cambridge – he makes worthwhile use. With the support of his people from top to bottom, if we are to believe the insistently panegyrical chorus, Hal makes moves to consolidate that support by winning a war against the French with minimal English losses. Using the power that patriarchal authority supplies him with, he manages successfully to harness the forces of violence of England and direct them at France. The whole military endeavour is a carefully contrived ritual of righteous slaughter whereby the king's power is firmly cemented. The battles are suffused with the language, ceremony and rites of violence. Like young Prince Hal's oathtaking before his father on the eve of the battle of Shrewsbury, the battles of Henry V are informed with a language and gesture of sanctity that represent the war as a quasi-holy enterprise destined to be entrenched in English history and mythology. Thus, the play comes to constitute an example of the potential efficacy of violence when it is the instrument solely of the legally and morally sanctioned authority. Though the play's own challenges to that authority are not sufficient to topple the mythologized king, they do assert the presence of an inherent moral contradiction informing the marriage of violence to a patriarchal politics.

In this tetralogy, women are located almost entirely in the realm of the 'other'. With the ambiguous exception of the Queen in *Richard II*, the women of these plays participate in a world that

seeks to subvert the official world of power. From the passionate Duchesses of Gloucester and York to the wives of Hotspur,
Mortimer, and Northumberland, to the tavern's Hostess Quickly
and Doll Tearsheet to Katherine of France, the visible positions of
the women are in opposition to the womanless patriarchal court. In
the present three tragedies, on the other hand, the women are central
figures in the patriarchal process which, ironically, depends upon
and takes its form from them. The women of patriarchy are a means
whereby the system expresses itself. Thus, in *Titus Andronicus*, the
rape of Lavinia, itself an assault on the valuation of fathers, is
avenged in an action that attempts to recuperate the authority of
the threatened society. Concomitant with Titus's gruesome revenge
comes the most expressive act of all, the killing of his own daughter,
a self-acknowledged guilty victim of rape. The complex of meanings
associated with her killing alludes directly to the patriarchal values
that are jeopardised by the fact that she has been raped.

Female chastity is the cornerstone of patriarchy, yet it cannot ultimately be controlled by men. In the end female sexual behaviour,
including female sexual desire, is under the sway of the individual
woman. This is the fact which threatens the basis of patriarchy and
which that system struggles to come to terms with. But the need to
control women is so dominant because the submission of women is
necessary to the survival of the system. The murder of Desdemona
is consciously associated by Othello with the survival of patriarchy.
He asserts that it is necessary lest she betray more men. When he
does finally kill her, of course, she has wakened and ceased to be
the acquiescent sacrificial object of his patriarchal longing; she is
instead a real woman with a real will to live. Recognizing her
as such, Othello unleashes into his violent act of killing a host
of terrible fears that make of the calmly constructed patriarchal
rationalization or 'cause' a dreadful, complex, psychologically and
physically chaotic act of violence. And yet, in the murder of his
wife, like Titus in the murder of his daughter, Othello expresses
the logic of the patriarchal structure of values. These men are tied
to the ideology of suppression as tightly as are the women they
suppress. Because of this, it is only reasonable for the women to
be objects of suspicion within the purview of that ideology. It can
become tragically necessary to kill them.

It is harder to make sense of the killing of Cordelia. Her murder
is committed by an anonymous soldier, a captain in the English
army on orders from Edmund. She does not know the man who

kills her; he does not know Cordelia. Her murder is supposed to be accompanied by the murder of Lear. In a sense this killing is merely a part of the random, bloody destruction that overwhelms the drama. Yet here too the fatal structure of patriarchal oppression looms. In many ways Cordelia is the most subversive of the three women. As Desdemona and Lavinia appear to accept patriarchy, to desire absorption by it, Cordelia, from her first words in the play, offers a qualified challenge to its principle premiss – the subjugation of the female self to the male. Cordelia's refusal halts the process in its tracks. She will not subsume her desire, her very identity, to that of a man, even if he is a beloved father. In the working out of the calamitous consequences of her choice, Cordelia occupies occasionally ambiguous ground in relation to the forces that finally kill her. Yet it is certain that one thing that does cause her death is her sex. The threat that she offers to the structure of patriarchal integrity is greater than the threat a man could offer. As a woman in courageous opposition to the political stability of an absolutist patriarchal monarchy, her adversity could hardly be greater or more menacing. It pits the logic of moderation against the logical extension of patriarchal power. Her death is a resolution at least to the problem of opposition. The Cordelia of Nahum Tate, safely married to Edgar, is a travesty of the dignified and integrated Cordelia Shakespeare gave us and a predictable and safely conservative vindication of the patriarchy Shakespeare's heroine throws off balance, if only for a moment.

Patriarchy defines and justifies itself according to categories – usually the relative categories of power. Gender and class structures provide the bases for the hierarchical differences upon which patriarchy depends and whose permutations and contradictions the previously mentioned plays explore and expose. *Macbeth* is the play of Shakespeare which comes closest to the point of breakdown of difference. The violence of that play assumes a momentum of its own, a momentum which carries it as close to the annihilation of these differences as it seems possible for drama to take us. *Macbeth* is, then, the subject of the conclusion of this study; it incorporates and extends many of the transgressive energies of the other plays and violently relocates them outside the realm of patriarchal forms. Ultimately the centrality of patriarchy in *Macbeth* too restates itself in the restoration of its structures.

2

The Containment
of Monarchy: *Richard II*

The cruelest irony of *Richard II* is the way in which the normally deforming political acts of assassination and revolution are pressed into the service of a political system that remains intact. The personal and political upheavals of the drama, superficially managed and controlled by rigorously formal verse, ultimately reproduce the structure of authority which created the usurpation in the first place. The play explores a power struggle in society's upper reaches. Some use is made – by Bolingbroke especially – of the ordinary citizens, but their relation to the battle for ascendancy is decidedly marginal. Yet that very marginality has its value in fleshing out a picture which, in a conservative critical tradition, has often been seen to contain only two 'great men' fighting over a throne. The unseen brace of draymen who bid Godspeed to Bolingbroke on his way to exile, perform in their gesture an act of political rebellion against their monarch. It is an act which fortifies and encourages Bolingbroke and which may thus be seen to have enabled rather than disturbed monarchy itself.

After the deposition 'rude misgovern'd hands from window tops / Threw dust and rubbish on King Richard's head' (V,ii,5–6). The notional presence of such spectacles in the play reinforces the disquiet that pervades the play, not least in the last scene where Bolingbroke's occupation of the throne mocks Richard's by being so like it. Yet their modest presence as reported gestures – support for the king's enemy and vilification of the king – refers to the existence of tacit subversive potential inherent in the ideology of divinely ordained monarchy which Richard desperately attempts to foster as his reign founders. Tennenhouse argues that Bolingbroke's rebellious momentum supplies the play with a carnivalesque element not offered by the oppressed subjects of the play, and that in this way the political forces of the drama are fully contained within the traditional patriarchal structure. He suggests, further, that 'the history plays all turn on this use of the materials of carnival. The popular energy embodied in carnival legitimizes authority, provided that energy can be incorporated in the political body of the state.'[1] The ordinary people of this play – those who have no acknowledged political power – turn their collective energy towards one or another of their potential *rulers* as the only allowable or recognizable form of political expression made available to them. Thus their political power becomes absorbed and expressed by the more powerful actual or potential rulers.

In this play the real subversive forces are very much in the background, reported rather than staged, heard rather than seen, shadowy presences whose existence touches but never changes the direction of events. For the events of the play are centred upon two men whose success and failure depend upon the credibility of their separate versions of monarchical power. Public disaffection is hinted at in the common people's cheering Bolingbroke and jeering at Richard, but the anger is directed at Richard himself rather than at monarchy. Indeed, the 'ordinary' citizens actually seen in the play, like the Gardener and his helper or the Servingman, actively enable the monarchical order through their criticism of Richard's abuses, making possible the easy transition from one ruler to the next. The Gardener, for example, is positively enthusiastic in his passion for monarchical absolutism. The conflicting forces by which the drama is played out conspire simultaneously to produce and resist violent disruption with the least possible disturbance. The result of the play's muted dialectic is a self-reflexive drama that advances the processes of pro- and retrospectivity. *Richard II* keeps tugging us with its own characters towards its centre. The last scene is an expression of futile nostalgia, self-pity and regret. Helplessly the king mourns the man whose death he has caused. The irony of the trap he finds himself in – a rigidly circumscribed monarchical system which produced the means of its own decapitation – is manifest in this final posture. The play offers the retrospective insight that medieval absolutism recognized no alternatives to itself while it laboured painfully under the sway of impulses towards change. The social classes acknowledged in the play are divided according to power and powerlessness. But, in this case, the opposition is not what Althusser would call a 'ruptural principle' necessary to a revolution; that is, it does not possess the elements or circumstances

capable of activating an assault on the ruling classes.[2] The forces
of revolution, with the assistance of a ubiquitous medievalism,
are thoroughly contained. Thus the political parameters of this
play are flattened and narrowed so as to disinclude the prospect
of revolutionary rupture. This is obviously not always the case
in Shakespeare's plays; here however, the drama seems bent on
producing an effect of power within a context of immobile absolutism. The contradiction inherent in the political confines of the play,
though an animating force, does not produce profound political
upheaval; rather it is absorbed and contained by many things,
including the presence of what Tennenhouse – after Bakhtin - calls
the carnivalesque. In proposing that carnival defuses the prospect of
revolution throughout the histories, however, Tennenhouse seems
to me not to allow for the genuine revolutionary potential adumbrated in *Henry IV* and *Henry V,* and discussed in later chapters.
These plays are different from *Richard II* precisely in that carnival
is an inadequate safeguard against revolutionary impulses, and
violence or the threat of violence alone is necessary to contain the
ruptural energy of revolution. In other words it is not carnivalesque
inversion that defuses popular discontent in, say, *Henry IV,* but
ruthless ideological imposition of the will of the ruling class and
the concomitant fear it engenders.

Shakespeare's medievalism, one of the truly powerful forces of
containment of *Richard II,* is as evident a means of legitimizing
authority as carnival. The medievalism takes a variety of forms
in the play, including, notoriously, arcane ritual, incantation, and
intensely regulated language. Bolingbroke's incantatory banishment of Exton, for example, constitutes the disposition of the most
visible reminder of the blood that covers the throne. But in that
banishment the new order reveals its means of absorbing and
appropriating political deformations to its own uses. Exton, the
agent of Bolingbroke's ambition, must depart so that the new king
can reassemble the fragmented forms of order under his own reign.
To validate the new monarchy, the exile of Exton is ritualized as an
eternal punishment. Exton becomes a classic scapegoat wherein the
monarch, by the magical and priestly exercise of his religious and
political authority, displaces social disruption. As the recognized
murderer of the king, Exton comes to embody political disintegration. Thus is Bolingbroke's 'revolution' contained and monarchy
restored. Bolingbroke's disposition of Exton is an attempt to recoup
the moral authority shattered by the usurpation.

With Cain go wander thorough shades of night,
And never show thy head by day nor light.
Lords, I protest my soul is full of woe
That blood should sprinkle to make me grow.
Come mourn with me for what I do lament,
And put on sullen black incontinent.
I'll make a voyage to the Holy Land,
To wash this blood from off my guilty hand.
March sadly after, grace my mournings here
In weeping after this untimely bier.

(V,vi,43–52)[3]

The disposition, like most decisions in his life so far, is a gamble. Bolingbroke uses the appropriative power of ambiguity and reflexiveness. The new king is less different from the brash young combatant he once was than is sometimes thought. In the early scenes of challenge, Bolingbroke showed himself adept at making moral, and hence political, capital out of his rage. Here he uses grief for similar purposes. With this speech Bolingbroke develops a strategy of ambiguity designed to invite misinterpretion. It becomes a powerful weapon in his rebellion and against further disruption. It is not, therefore, surprising that the critical literature on the play has underscored the lack of resolution offered by the play's conclusion: is the conclusion a guilty expiation or a mark of practical wisdom? As the authoritative figure of the drama, he has appropriated the power to determine the history of the events: he chooses publicly to mystify Richard's death with rhetorical and moralistic strategies. He invokes a potent biblical myth, he adumbrates a future of contrition, he protests his woe and proclaims his tears. He is, however, inescapably compromised by the mere fact of his audience. His motive is connected with the containment of the forces of opposition by which he has himself been able to reach the throne. Bolingbroke's great achievement is to have wrested substitution from revolution. He has captured the throne with only minor political disturbance and minimal social upheaval. The structures of monarchy – and vital, immanent contradiction – remain intact and are vividly exemplified by his forgiveness of Aumerle.

The failure of Henry IV to acknowledge his crime fully – the following plays are full of vacillation between accusation and self-justification – is another of his means of securing an endangered throne. Moody Prior's assertion, typical of many readings of this moment, that at this point, the 'alternative to Bolingbroke is political chaos',[4] is directly complicitous with Bolingbroke's own position. In his use of the mythology of kingship and a universal hunger for stability, the king has made his subjects acknowledge that there is no workable alternative rule to his own. By taking power, Bolingbroke has reproduced the conditions that made it possible for him to take the throne in the first place. Patriarchy remains the entrenched political structure and revolution has been disabled. And although, of course, differences of personality and political style exist within any patriarchal monarchy, the use of power and the limits upon that use are circumscribed by historical and cultural factors. Indeed, it can be argued that the events represented in the two following Henry plays confirm the point. If the play's ending is a dark mirror-image of the beginning, then the text dominates its participants and observers in a forceful way. It compels retrospectivity. We do not have the luxury of looking forward in tranquillity as we have learned to do after the apparently ordered – or re-ordered – conclusions of most Shakespearean tragedies. Readings of *Richard II* are fairly unanimous in their recognition that the play fails, or refuses, to yield a solution to the problems of monarchy that it produces. Its conflict of values, says Norman Rabkin, is an 'unresolved thematic issue'.[5] Its tragedy, he notes elsewhere, is the 'complementarity of its protagonists' virtues, which seem . . . incapable of being commingled.'[6] Such a reading of the situation at the end fits the sense that the killing of the king and his courtiers has changed very little in the polity; that the differences between the two kings as men – as bodies natural – have little importance for the lives of their subjects; that Bolingbroke has achieved his goal of substituting himself for Richard and, finally, that essential disturbance within the body politic has been contained. The disposition of Exton is above all a gesture of political consolidation. Though it has been argued that revolution *per se* has no ideological viability in this play, the constantly expressed anxiety about order is, as well, fear of an assault on the ruling class and the concomitant fear of the substitution of a government which does not protect that class from the undefined class which would replace it. Concealment of anxiety takes the shape of a conspiracy of the ruling class in the drama. Ambiguity and indirection become powerful instruments of government.

The first lines of the play, like the last, reveal an attempt to conceal the threat of fragmentation and ambivalence by the super-application of a uniform discursive system. That system, evident in language, action, and gesture, is the crux of monarchy in the drama. Maintaining the *appearance* of political stability is a powerful motive for both Richard and Bolingbroke. The ceremoniousness which Tillyard discovered almost everywhere in the play is one of the means by which discord can be disguised or forestalled, contradiction effaced.[7] Jonathan Goldberg's discussion of the contrasting monarchical styles of Elizabeth and James – the 'style of *Gods*' – is a discussion, ultimately of their discursive dramatic modes: Elizabeth, an active participant in the processes of power, James, a detached, imperial animator.[8] Richard's mode is the mode of imperial manipulation. The monarch can dictate and determine the style of his monarchy. And in that determination resides an enormous deal of his authority. Richard's first speech, an example of his political practice, establishes the nature of his power; the ritual he implies in his mode of speaking is confirmed by his respondents. It signifies that at the end of the drama, for all his apparent attempts to disrupt the monarchical practice of Richard, Bolingbroke's speech, quoted above, is largely a surrender to the acknowledged monarchical mode by being an imitation of it. We see Richard asserting this power at the outset of the play.

> Old John of Gaunt, time-honored Lancaster,
> Hast thou according to thy oath and band
> Brought hither Henry Herford thy bold son,
> Here to make good the boist'rous late appeal,
> Which then our leisure would not let us hear,
> Against the Duke of Norfolk, Thomas Mowbray?
>
> (I,i,1–6)

The occasion itself eloquently answers the question. And yet, within the formal rhetoric of the question the word 'boist'rous' sounds a warning note. Its curious informality and nonconformity within the passage produce a definite, if momentary, rhetorical dislocation that subverts the smoothness of the ceremonial language. Harry Berger argues that the word here in combination with 'son' tends to 'diminish Bolingbroke – to *boy* him – and to stress Gaunt's responsibility for his son's good behaviour'.[9] Richard's sense of his authority is expressed through his style. The lines suggest a recognition of tension and the presence of a threat. The gloss of latinate pomp is pierced by the sound of 'boy'. The king's use of ritual and the phrases of ceremony are exposed *as* use by the evidence of conflict. The question indicates progress through time to a new phase of action; for all that the answer is already known, the question indicates an unresolved circumstance. The need to put the question is a subtle means of incorporating and acknowledging the power of the public for whose sake it is put, just as Bolingbroke's final speech, addressed to 'my lords', is a means of including his audience as tacit accomplices in his last act, while he makes acknowledgement of his partial dependence on them. There are common motives in the play's first and last speeches, though they are spoken by different kings.

Richard's next speech more fully exposes the generalized disquiet which the first question hinted at, and more completely links Richard in his uneasy occupation of the throne with Bolingbroke in his final scene as an uncertain and fearful king.

> Tell me, moreover, hast thou sounded him,
> If he appeal the Duke on ancient malice,
> Or worthily as a good subject should
> On some known ground of treachery in him?
>
> (I,i,8–11)

Once again, the rhetoricity of the question discloses, as it attempts to conceal, a disturbance by leading us forward to a forthcoming response. The attempt at compact stylization only heightens the tension of the moment. Notwithstanding the majestic dominance of the questioner, the question takes its dramatic and rhetorical power from the words 'malice' and 'treachery', terms which directly threaten majesty. The brittleness of the ceremony intensifies with Richard's construction of the conflict in increasingly violent terms – 'High-stomach'd', 'full of ire', 'In rage, deaf as the sea' (I,i,18–19) – which carefully exclude his own relation to it. As that relation is made more explicit with the unfolding events, Richard becomes increasingly tied to a situation from which he is vainly attempting to keep a distance.

The opening scene's Richard and the closing scene's Bolingbroke are startlingly alike. Robert Ornstein has noted some parallels between the kings: 'Like Richard [Bolingbroke] has shed a kinsman's blood; like Richard he fears rebellious subjects; and like Richard he banishes the follower who was his hangman.'[10] The two monarchs are politically committed to a language which is incapable of containing or defusing the inherent and potential dangers upon which their reigns are founded. The language itself is vulnerable by virtue of its heavy reliance on formality and its manifestly determined limitations. Bolingbroke's style is reported to include gestures that embrace the populace at large, but the participatory style does not last. When he is monarch, his speech becomes his vehicle of separation, a means of enforcing the difference between himself and his subjects. His ready adoption of the monarch's traditional rhetoric in such strategies as the royal 'we' and the directive and assertive use of commonplace symbols and myths indicate the triumph of the spirit of monarchy and of Richard's style. And yet as characters they are thoroughly different. The languid Richard is constantly counterposed with the 'manly' Bolingbroke. These opposing qualities ricochet off each other throughout the drama until the last act when Richard, facing death, grabs a weapon from one of the murderers and kills him, while Bolingbroke sits on his throne weakened and immobilized, capable, rather like the early Richard, of speech that issues from the painful awareness of conflicting internal stress. The substitution seems there to be complete, speaking as it does to the ways in which the discourse which the king adopts becomes his prison.

But between these reflexive ends are two scenes which stand as apparent attempts to resolve some of the conflicts of style and value and to reconcile the contradictions implicit in the ubiquitous concealments. These are the Gardener scene and the deposition scene. In each, rhetoric is augmented and intensified by emblematic actions which provide simplified ideological readings of the larger political and moral questions of the play. The apparent simplicity suggests an arbitrary and superimposed solution to a complex set of issues. To E. M. W. Tillyard the former scene is a mini-morality play where Shakespeare spells out his message of authoritative government; the Gardener scene stands as a clear declaration of the playwright's (and, it seems, Tillyard's own) political ideology. Tillyard calls the Gardener a 'just repressor of vices', who comprehends the 'proper relation' of things and 'the great principle of order'.[11] His *Richard II*, in other words, is monological and unambiguous. The deconstructionists, however, have taught us that the text is always there; that the Gardener is apprehended by his readers according to a politics and subjectivity that is already determined. The ambiguity of the play finds revealing expression in the incompatible ways in which this character has been made to support such readings as Tillyard's, where he 'stands for' order, and such as those readings which comprehend him as the embodiment of the play's indeterminacy and uncertainty. The imagery of the Gardener's speeches is surely an imagery of brutality and tyranny. His method of keeping his garden orderly is uncomfortably reminiscent of the brutal treatment which Bolingbroke accords Bushy and Green, whose heads are lopped off. Whether, however, we prefer to call the Gardener a just repressor or a tyrant, there remains about his political solutions a palpable directness and simplicity that stand in stark contrast to the uncertainty and nervousness of Richard and Bolingbroke whose views of political control include and attempt to account for disturbance and disaffection.

As she recognizes the Gardener, the queen wagers that the gardeners will 'talk of state, for everyone doth so, / Against a change' (III,iv,26–27). The dramatic flow is disrupted by a metadramatic moment. All who are not part of the play are directed to watch the play. Suddenly its 'playness' is foregrounded, with the result that the whole scene is lit with skepticism. Its language must be listened to not merely as ungardenerlike, but as an artificially produced discourse of performance whose relation to the fraught monarchy is proportional to that monarchy's relation to the playhouse. The dialogue which she overhears and the actions she observes are an enactment and a declaration of the principles of hierarchical government, a valorization of social order as an ultimate good and indirectly an espousal of Machiavellian political theories. The Gardener's first words are an order to one of his servants to 'bind up young dangling apricocks' (28). The Gardener himself is subordinate to the queen and defers to her as he was deferred to by his man. That is, the actions of the episode mimic the sense of its speeches. But the several examples of perfect deference in the scene bear no relation to the conflicts which have caused the tragic events of the play. The Gardener and his two menservants are the most powerless characters actually present in the play. Ordinary life is subject to the same systems of order as life on the highest political levels – government by fear. For while the Gardener's speeches seem to refer to the garden and, by extension, the commonwealth itself, they also betray anxiety about insurrection by the labouring poor to be found frequently in Elizabethan writings. The Gardener's directions stress the need for legitimate forms of violence as a means of maintaining order in society. His language is direct and oddly brutal, his imagery that of political tyranny. Though for purposes of allegory he is a gardener, his magisterial, ruthless language stamps

him as a successful tyrant. Better yet, he is a successful monarch
who rules by the word. Remote, aloof, yet in control, his sovereignty
depends upon his mysterious knowledge of his craft:

> Go thou, and like an executioner
> Cut of the heads of too fast growing sprays.
>
> (33–4)

Bushy, Bagot, and Green are the noisome weeds and caterpillars so
harshly dealt with by Bolingbroke, the validity of whose charges
against them is asseverated rather than demonstrated. Indeed,
though one of Bolingbroke's most potent charges against them is
that they have

> Made a divorce betwixt his queen and him,
> Broke the possession of a royal bed,
> And stain'd the beauty of a fair queen's cheeks
> With tears, drawn from her eyes
>
> (III,112–15)

it is Bushy who offers the queen consolation in a dark hour (II,ii). It
is, as Tennenhouse suggests, part of Bolingbroke's strategy to make
Richard himself seem the enemy of monarchy, and the friend of
disintegration and 'divorce'.[12] The memory of their last courageous
appearances subverts the authority of the Gardener's depiction of
them and, hence, of the events he describes and principles he
adumbrates. Kristian Smidt notes that Richard's flatterers are not
shown to be wicked, and argues that 'practically all our impression
of misrule is derived from his critics and enemies'.[13] In the garden
scene the text narrows its focus to a set of simple and concentrated
ideas, specifics, and remedies for political, social, and individual
ills. They assume highly centralized power structures and a ruthless
disregard for individual liberty. That is, when 'monarchy' actually
succeeds, as it seems to have done in the garden, it fails as badly
as it does in the hands of Richard or Bolingbroke. For ideally it is
more than the containment of power, the maintenance of political
control. The play bursts with idealizations of monarchical values –
Gaunt, York, Carlisle give passionate defenses of its virtues – but in
its examples and allegories it shows monarchy only as tyranny. The
Gardener mythologizes the maintenance of power through a series
of ideologically charged images – natural, medical, horticultural,
biblical – which make violent solutions morally and socially valid:

> We at time of year
> Do wound the bark, the skin of our fruit trees,
> Lest, being over-proud in sap and blood,
> With too much riches it confound itself;
> Had he done so to great and growing men,
> They might have liv'd to bear , and he to taste
> Their fruits of duty. Superfluous branches
> We lop away, that bearing boughs may live
>
>   (57–64)

The anti-naturalistic representations of the scene – its language and stylized gestures – contribute to its authority, while its context and rhetorical modes undermine that authority; these subversive features help expose an underlying turbulence which its elevated emblematism cannot conceal. Stephanie Jed notes the centrality of the metaphor to the ideology of political tyranny in the humanistic tradition. The Gardener's example of decapitation follows an ideological practice which finds metaphorical stories about political violence central to its own concerns.[14]

That turbulence is at the heart of the play. It resides in the ultimate inability of language to recover moral and political stability from the wastes of discord inherent in the hierarchical structure of the 'England' of *Richard II*. The Gardener scene shows that within such a structure authority is vulnerable when ruthlessness becomes random and disorderly or, equally, when the metaphors of order depart from their frames in a universal system. Yet ruthlessness is a byproduct of monarchy. As the Gardener orders the lopping off of the heads of weeds, so Bolingbroke has lopped off the heads of Bushy and Greene, and Richard has beheaded Gloucester (II,ii,102). According to the Gardener, Richard has too often departed from the rules of order, and so – according to the ideology – nature itself has taken revenge on him. This way of thinking implies a formal construction of nature as possessed of a malevolent impulse to destroy the world of man which seeks to tame it – the kingdom is dystopia. It is a notion to which Richard himself subscribes as when, on his return from Ireland, he conjures the earth to release its malevolent force and destroy his enemies:

> Yield stinging nettles to mine enemies;
> And when they from thy bosom pluck a flower,

> Guard it I pray thee, with a lurking adder
>
> (III,ii,18–20)

C. H. Herford aptly describes Richard in this crisis as creating 'a fairyland.'[15] And John Baxter discusses the speech as an example of Richard's 'libertine golden style'. The phrase nicely refers to the self-indulgent, simplistic ideology to which the king resorts at this moment. 'Richard's golden style, successful for depicting his own intense feeling, is too free, too private and too idiosyncratic to enrich his moral understanding.'[16] We might add that this style is reflective of his self-destructive penchant for modes of construction that too easily and concretely find simple analogical patterns in the natural world.

The contradictions inherent in the ideological forms of hierarchical government are exposed most clearly through the dramatic processes of the deposition scene. There the participants are confronted with the evidence of the contradiction in the simultaneous occupation of the stage by the two kings with evidently equal claims to the throne. Dramatic form is given to the process of political fragmentation as the scene closes with a fresh set of conspirators revealing themselves in a common desire to 'rid the realm of this pernicious blot' (IV,i,325). That moment is directly reflective of an earlier scene. Richard's most flamboyantly divisive act is his seizure of Bolingbroke's land at Gaunt's death. As he departs the stage, Northumberland, Ross, and Willoughby reveal their disaffection. Rabkin has usefully pointed out that the immediate motive for Bolingbroke's plot is demonstrably *not* the king's seizure of Bolingbroke's land since, as Northumberland confides, even before his father's death Bolingbroke was armed and on his way back to England:[17]

> If then we shall shake off our slavish yoke,
> Imp out our drooping country's broken wing,
> Redeem from broking pawn the blemish'd crown,
> Wipe off the dust that hides our sceptre's gilt,
> And make high majesty look like itself.
>
> (II,i,291–5)

In the scene of deposition the consequences of usurpation are spelled out. The deposition commences in an atmosphere of brutality which is represented as a byproduct of the historical impulses of a patriarchal culture in which violence has lost its purpose. That purpose, as the Gardener scene has so forcefully reminded us, is the maintenance of order through the advancement of hierarchical authority. Moments before Richard enters – under arrest – Carlisle has been arrested and sentenced for his 'pains'. (IV,i,150) In its way, Carlisle's speech is as narrowly focussed and cliche-ridden as the Gardener's. Carlisle's passion is given full voice in his prophecy:

> And if you crown him, let me prophesy –
> The blood of English shall manure the ground,
> And future ages groan for this foul act.

> (136–8)

But, in a sense, the prophecy has already come to pass. The 'figure of God's majesty, / His captain, steward, deputy elect' (125–6) has long been king, and the result has been largely 'this house' raised 'against this house' (145). The quasi-mystical religious authority that Carlisle brings to his speech does not efface its biases in favour of a conventional patriarchal politics. Carlisle's speech, and other presentations of the royalist position, Prior reminds us, 'arise out of the dramatic circumstances, and if the play is a storehouse of passages relating to divine right it need not follow that their cumulative force necessarily produces a favourable response to the idea'.[18]

Richard is conducted into the presence of Bolingbroke by his uncle York, the character who embodies the reflexiveness of the play. York, by his own declaration, is loyal to the king of England and has attempted in vain to play an unambiguous part in this tragedy of ideologies. But, in the end, the political alternatives from which he believes he must choose are both ideologies of self-interest. Each promises to help him keep what power he has. Bolingbroke is emphatically not a new broom, not a revolutionist bent on changing or breaking structures of power. He is a substitute monarch whose hardest task is plastering over the cracks he has caused by usurpation, legitimizing an illegal reign gained by murder. The success of his usurpation depends upon his ability to continue the existing conditions of hierarchy and patriarchy after violently grasping control of them; the loyalty of his powerful allies is largely conditional on his fidelity to their notions of government.

Such contradictions and philosophical convolutions are the subject of Richard's most piercing recognitions. He taunts Bolingbroke with the irreconcilability of the situation, the contradiction that cannot be erased even by murder. For in the political scheme of this world of power, murder becomes the logical means of reconciling the irreconcilable; it is a procrustean attempt to resolve through violence what cannot be resolved through logic.

As he enters the stage which has been set for his deposition Richard lays bare the paradox:

> Alack, why am I sent for to a king
> Before I have shook off the regal thoughts
> Wherewith I reign'd?
>
> (IV,i,164–6)

He has precisely and pragmatically identified the problem. Two kings of England occupy the stage; those present can be subjects of only one of them, must betray one of them. There has been a radical shift in Richard's position. The space he now occupies he occupies under entirely other and new political conditions. His discourse embodies new terms and terminologies. So profound is the upheaval, so changed the context of his world, that nothing he says, however familiar, can be tied to old assumptions.

The struggle of this play is largely a battle of the contending parties to control the formation of ideology. Each antagonist claims the same ideological allegiance. Each, however, hopes to define his own version of that ideology as the moral and practical one. Richard loses in large measure because he and his adherents are too ideologically pure, too devoted to monarchy as a moral credo. Bolingbroke's questionable success, dependent to be sure upon Richard's failure, is also a result of his capacity to persuade his followers, from the lords to the draymen, that his version of monarchy will better succeed in bringing them peace and prosperity. The scene that follows culminates in the disclosure that the new king's more powerful subjects are ready to dethrone him. As Bolingbroke and his followers exit, a new conspiracy is articulated among Carlisle, the Abbot of Westminster and Aumerle, a conspiracy that is the counterpart and repetition, with variations, of the earlier conspiracy which involved Northumberland, Ross and Willoughby.

Reflexiveness achieves a kind of climax in the mirror episode, but that is only its final and most subtle expression. From the moment Richard appears a dividedness of vision impels the attention of all present, on- and offstage spectators alike. The words of the scene are hurled back and forth between Richard and Bolingbroke; even those which involve others always refer to the two antagonists. Northumberland is a convenient conduit for harshness, for *realpolitik*, but his dramatic purpose is to exacerbate the tension between the monarch and his opposite. Though he does disturb Richard, he is included in this text not as a source of disturbance so much as a means of underscoring the pragmatic realities and consequences of the event.

The event itself is a coming to terms with the brutal ideological forms whose political and subject logic has led to this dismantling of the self. Richard divests himself of a good deal more than the crown in this scene. He attempts here to expose the multiplicity of structures by which that self is created and, in doing so, becomes increasingly aware of patterns of opposition which make it seem whole. And then, in a dramatic and suggestive gesture, he explodes the structures themselves as essentially patternless. In that gesture Richard repudiates the meanings of the symbols and ideologies by which he has identified and understood who he is.

In the exchanges between Richard and Bolingbroke the personal pronouns predominate. Indeed, as Joseph Porter notes, throughout the play Richard's speech is overwhelmingly dominated by the first person.[19] Richard, whose self-references were habitually made through the traditional royal *we*, has become *I* with a vengeance. His focus has narrowed remarkably to a self-identification that recognizes and presents a single self. But it is nevertheless a single self that derives from the undeniable presence of an opposite – Bolingbroke, the man whose existence determines his presence:

> Now mark me how I will undo myself . . .
> With mine own tears I wash away my balm,
> With mine own hands I give away my crown . . .
> All pomp and majesty I do forswear . . .
> God save King Henry, unking'd Richard says,
> And send him many years of sunshine days!
>
> (203–21)

This speech reverses the 'doing' of a self. It inverts the structural patterns which have gone into the creation of an identity. Richard enumerates the very forms and ritualized ideologies by which he has been stabilized, and in doing so exposes their essential hollowness, their essentially illusory nature. He reveals his life as a

kind of literary text, artificially unified by superimposed structures
and culturally determined meanings.

To the moment when he breaks the mirror Richard clings to
the illusions of patriarchy. He describes and defines his suffering according to a range of mythologies which give it a kind of
formal presence and a rhetorical power. His desire for death is
patterned upon the powerful myth of martyrdom in which he
presents his own demise as more tragic and lonely than that of
Jesus – 'But he, in twelve, / Found truth in all but one; I, in
twelve thousand, none' (170–1). In doing this, in hyperbolizing
his own betrayal, he makes a palpable use of mythology. Having
'undecked' himself, Richard seems to search through the ruins for
a remaining self which he finds on his own 'sour cross' (241). James
Calderwood has objected that 'instead of dignifying Richard as he
surely intends it to do the association forces him to suffer an
impossible comparison'.[20]

The undoing leads to the almost literally blinding perceptions
of the mirroring effect that his tears create. Looking into himself
because his tears have blinded him, forced his vision inwards,
Richard recognizes his own relation to the structure of usurpation,
its mythology makes innocence an illusion:

> Mine eyes are full of tears, I cannot see.
> And yet salt water blinds them not so much
> But they can see a sort of traitors here.
> Nay, if I turn mine eyes upon myself,
> I find myself a traitor with the rest.
>
> (244–8)

In the 'traitors' around him, Richard sees the reflection of himself.
The ideologies of treachery and loyalty are all-encompassing – 'For
I have given here my soul's consent / T'undeck the pompous body
of a king' (249–51). The passion for oblivion that Richard exhibits
reflects his acknowledgement of the ultimate failure of cultural
forms to substantiate or codify the event. For in his representation
of oblivion Richard seems to seek an escape from the constraints
and limitations of the myths and forms from which he has derived
his sense of self.

Oblivion is, of course, as culturally determined a concept as
monarchism. It alludes to the possibility of formlessness, of a
kind of inchoate experience, released from the rigid ceremonies,

rituals and ideologies by which this king has been determined. The metaphor of oblivion –

> O that I were a mockery king of snow,
> Standing before the sun of Bolingbroke,
> To melt myself away in water-drops!
>
> (261–3)

represents a paradoxical, unachievable straining after a world of experience and language that might free the self from feelings which are tied to linguistically determined structures. What develops from the futility of this wish for non-being or, more likely, diffused being, is an inevitable subsequent recognition of its futility. This recognition leads to a dramatization of the notion through the play's narrative and its theatrical signs that rigid patriarchal political practice has close evolutionary links to violence as a mode of resolving its own contradictions. To Armstrong and Tennenhouse 'violent events are not simply so but are called violent because they bring together different concepts of social order'.[21] *Richard II* challenges this concept of violence in its representation of the same – hierarchical and patriarchal – concept of social order in violently opposed terms. Bolingbroke, in a sense, wants to *be* Richard, but can only succeed by seeming to be his opposite. The violence of the language of the play, straining as it does to break the bounds of rigid verse structures, derives from the attempt of each antagonist to propose himself as the opposite of the other. Richard as Christ is as artificial a construction as that of Bolingbroke as a calm conciliator.

The act of breaking the mirror is the fullest expression – to this point in the play – of this impulse towards difference. Richard's violence derives directly out of a kind of metonymizing. He sees his face in the mirror but speaks to his reflection as if it were in actual fact his face. The face becomes the correlative for the multiple forms of power and authority, the symbol of his monarchy, the evidence of his identity. Yet, as he notes, the various shapes represented by the reflection in the mirror are an illusion:

> Was this face the face
> That every day under his household roof
> Did keep ten thousand men? Was this the face
> That like the sun did make beholders wink?

Is this the face which fac'd so many follies,
That was at last out-fac'd by Bolingbroke?
A brittle glory shineth in this face;
As brittle as the glory is the face

                                                        (281–8)

The face – the word is repeated in different ways eight times in as
many lines – is, in fact, not the face but its reflection. Yet, what
Richard sees in the mirror, for all that it is an outward sign, is
the very essence of himself. The obsessive repetition of the word
centralizes the signifier in the text. The destruction of the face in
the glass is thus a recognition not merely of the illusion of power;
rather it is the destruction of the whole world around him in
a sudden demonstration of awareness of the irreconcilability of
the complex systems of contradiction which the face represents
and which the flung, whirling mirror captures. Richard's mortal
body and his role as king are separable. Richard becomes, with
the perception that forces him to break the mirror, the real radical
of the drama, the one person who gives voice to the idea that
monarchy is a political fraud. This notion is implicit in the actions
of usurper and conspirator alike, but it is the dethroned king who
puts it into his gestures and his words. Bolingbroke has finally
become the official spokesman for a conservative politics. He has
convinced his subjects that it is through him that the monarchy can
be stabilized and that Richard's way points to anarchy. Thus the
draymen and marginalized subjects of the monarchy become the
agents of a traditional hierarchical monarchy, whose disaffection for
Richard is a repudiation of change.

Bolingbroke's response to Richard's perception that his sorrow
has destroyed his face is a means of restoring practical monarchical
politics to its privileged place – he reverts to literalism:

The shadow of your sorrow hath destroy'd
The shadow of your face.

                                                        (292–3)

The words, which have been praised for exposing Richard's
histrionic gesture, have, however, the effect of an attempt to
deny or negate the recognitions inherent in Richard's violent
act. Bolingbroke's attempt to valorize literal, perceptible reality
as 'truth' is an attempt to resurrect the somewhat battered ideology

of patriarchy. He is maintaining the mystique of difference, for it is through the production of a representation of difference alone that he can achieve domination.

Bolingbroke's restoration of patriarchy through the agencies of literalism and formality is flimsy because Richard is still able, by voice and sheer presence, to contradict his assumptions. A basic means by which the patriarchal system is justified is the contradictory reference to its observable universality and its demonstrable truth. That 'truth' is, of course, based upon an assumption of the primacy of God which is itself an illusion made real by faith alone. Without the evidence that faith provides, the structure of patriarchy presented in this text – Carlisle's speech being perhaps its most potent example – is severely weakened.

Richard's mere presence during Bolingbroke's reign represents a serious political challenge to the *idea* of monarchy and all its mimetic institutions within the society. It is devastating evidence of the contradictions of the system by which 'England' is governed and by which it survives. Thus it is that Richard must be killed. His death as presented in the text resonates beyond its conclusion, beyond the words of defeat uttered at that conclusion by the present king. His death and Bolingbroke's occupation of the throne represent a very substantial resolution of the conflicts of the play. But they are a resolution unlikely to provide simple moral instructions on how to view the play's problems. The events of the last two scenes alert us to the extent of this world's need of resolution at any cost. The violent death of a lineal king is the cost of the maintenance of patriarchy, of the monarchy which is uncritically acknowledged as the only available or acceptable form of government. The implication of dominance within the monarchical ideal, however benignly that ideal is represented, is never separable from the methodology of violence.

Richard's mode of dying complicates the issue – as the dying of all tragic heroes complicates it – by his very resistance to death simultaneously with his embrace of it. His keeper must taste his food: when he is assaulted by the murderers he resists them. His last words are an ultimate act of faith in the very system that has betrayed him and a repudiation of his radical insights. He movingly asserts his royalty, deriving solace, it seems, from the very ideologies he has thrown into question. The last speech of Richard is passionately atavistic in its reversions. It is in his death, says Terry Eagleton, that he finds 'his most accomplished theatrical moment. Something comes of nothing, as Richard wrests his most elaborate fiction from the process of being dismantled':[22]

> Exton, thy fierce hand
> Hath with the king's blood stain'd the king's own land.
> Mount, mount, my soul! thy seat is up on high,
> Whilst my gross flesh sinks downward, here to die.
>
> (V,v,109–12)

But the atavism only attests to the power that ideology exerts over the mind. The last words of a dying man are invested with a mystique revered and respected in most cultures. The dying man himself, tragedy demonstrates time and again, values his own dying words as greatly as his hearers can. Like them, he recognizes the need to justify and order his life as he leaves it. This impulse is part and parcel of the universal denaturalization of death. Richard is no less a victim/practitioner of this process than anyone else. Certainly he is no less so than Bolingbroke himself, who dwells on his own death with histrionic self-consciousness in his last moments. Richard's words carry authority, in part, because they are his last words. They bear heavily down on his successor, Henry of Lancaster. Exton presents Richard's body to the king as breathless – incapable of speech – as his buried fear; as the mightiest of his greatest enemies. Richard's death is a political advantage for Bolingbroke but a dramatic advantage for Richard. His murder testifies to his endurance beyond the bounds of the text. Bolingbroke on the other hand looms over the conclusion, presiding over the play's end, but defeated by it. He is irresolute, depressed, certain of nothing so much as Richard's greater greatness than his own.

3

The Legitimation of Violence in *1 Henry IV*

The violence of *2 Henry IV* is, ultimately, confined to the tavern. That of *Richard II* and *1 Henry IV* belongs to the court. In all cases the style of the violence serves an important political purpose. The violence of the tavern serves to remind the audiences, readers, and spectators, who are also citizens and subjects, that unlawful violence must be contained and subject to lawful violence, which is the instrument of authority. The violence of the court, of the rich and powerful, is or is transformed into axiomatically lawful violence. *1 Henry IV* is a demonstration of how lawful violence is shaped into an enabling instrument of authority, how it is legalized and made to supply a social need. Indeed, as I shall argue, the narrative of the play concentrates in large part on glorifying physical violence as a necessary force of morality. It needs to be said that the play does this in conformity with the secular and sacred historical traditions from which it issues. An underlying irony of *1 Henry IV* is the contingent knowledge that though the dominant authority possesses and asserts – as always – the right to define the value of violence and the social good, this throne has recently been gained by usurpation; the play covers a situation where Hotspur and his allies are challenging the legitimacy of that very power of ideological appropriation on behalf of Mortimer, whose claim to the throne is clearly stronger than King Henry's. The presence of this irony is a constant challenge to the official politics of the court.

Initially the violence of *1 Henry IV* has an unclear focus. The king's admiration of Hotspur is admiration of his prowess as a warrior. There are several good fighters on the rebel side, including Glendower, and several people are praised for their soldierly ability. But all of this fighting leads to disorder and confusion. However, in the story of Prince Hal is concentrated the socially useful idea of the possibility of violence being good – moral, legitimate, and, even, sacred. That story moves us from a situation in which violence is seen to be undirected, illegitimate, broken and random, to a situation in which its purpose has been discovered and its agent purified.

The ending of *Richard II* is crucial for this narrative. The stunned, unhappy conclusion of that play with the king's futile effort to expiate his act of violence is an essential effect for the beginning of *1 Henry IV*. The sense of hopelessness in *Richard II* is followed by an observable attempt at the beginning of the next play to harness violence. The play commences in bloodshed and confusion. King Henry's first speech is a mass of artificial optimism, concealment, contradiction and manufactured irony.

> So shaken as we are, so wan with care,
> Find we a time for frighted peace to pant,
> And breathe short-winded accents of new broils
> To be commenc'd in stronds afar remote:
> No more the thirsty entrance of this soil
> Shall daub her lips with her own children's blood,
> No more shall trenching war channel her fields,
> Nor bruise her flow'rets with the armed hoofs
> Of hostile paces.
>
> (I,i,1–9)

For him the only available means for rectifying this situation is the means of violence. Throughout the play on all levels, violence and force are valorized. They are the enabling instruments of power. The play is full of stirring tales of the use of violence, of cowardice in the face of it, of facing violent death and fleeing from it. But all these interspersed narratives and the initial confusions of the play swirl around a rather still centre. Prince Hal is the secret, unknown and undiscovered agent of violent destruction. His greatest weapon is surprise, the fact that he is undiscovered. His story, largely separated from that of the intrigue of the court, is a story of emergence into the sunlight through the ritualization and sanctification of a widely perceived and presented need to impose order on society through the demonstrable possession of a superior capacity to exercise violence.

The value, indeed the need, of ritual purification through violent action, is an obsessive and haunting theme of King Henry's reign. His first speech refers to the dream of levying an English power

> To chase these pagans in those holy fields
> Over whose acres walked those blessed feet
> Which fourteen hundred years ago we nail'd
> For our advantage on the bitter cross
>
> (I,i,24–7)

The violence of the image is hidden in a discourse of religious fervour. It contrasts tellingly with the description of the defeat of Mortimer who, fighting in the king's behalf,

> Against the irregular and wild Glendower,
> Was by the rude hands of that Welshman taken,
> A thousand of his people butchered,
> Upon whose dead corpse there was such misuse,
> Such beastly shameless transformation,
> By those Welshwomen done, as may not be
> Without much shame retold or spoken of.
>
> (I,i,40–7)

The barely disguised reference to the sexual mutilation of enemy corpses by the triumphant Welshwomen is a reference to another ritual of violence, one which possesses the overtones of magic rites, designed, perhaps, to rid Wales forever of the invader and his heirs. Westmoreland's description, however, is couched in the language of revulsion and disgust and completes a passage that pointedly distinguishes between good and evil violence and good and evil rituals of violence. There is, of course, another mutilation of a corpse in the play, and it too is a ritualized act of barbarity that stands as a kind of debasement or travesty of the rituals of socially beneficial violence. In these two acts of mutilation, however, the play intensifies the political divisions between beneficial and harmful violence. It is part of the larger discourse of power in this play to make real the distinction between kinds of violence, to impose on the nation a systematised authority which is supported by the court's superior physical force. The first scene shows the flailing, uncertain, and unsuccessful attempts of the monarch to supply that kind of authority. He is beleaguered and challenged on all sides.

The disintegrity of the central world is evident everywhere. The comicality of Hotspur in his first appearance intensifies the sense of fragmentation. This, after all, is the man whom the monarch has described as 'sweet Fortune's minion and her pride' (I,i,82). Yet, for all his military prowess, Hotspur is excessively loquacious and impetuous to the point that even his friends mock and despair of him.

But it is Hotspur, in the end, who is to be the means by which those broken rites of violence are to be restored. It is through him that the court is able to recover the means of government. It is Hotspur's power, reputation, and self-love that provide the court, through Prince Hal, with the ability to return to legalized sanctified authority. Though his career commences on a note of frantic comic frustration, it concludes in a moment of tragedy so poignantly realized as to have inspired Northrop Frye's perception that the warrior's dying remark, 'thoughts, the slaves of life', comes out of the heart of the tragic vision.[1] His life has been linked with that of Prince Hal from the first scene, their destinies have been welded together in anticipation of the final encounter. Each of their characters is molded by forces and events that centre on the great fact of violence at the heart of the play. Hotspur's final speech is a tragic acknowledgement of the convergence of their fates in the arena of violent struggle:

> O Harry, thou hast robb'd me of my youth!
> I better brook the loss of brittle life
> Than those proud titles thou hast won of me;
> They wound my thoughts worse than thy sword my flesh:
> But thoughts, the slaves of life, and life time's fool,
> And time that takes survey of all the world,
> Must have a stop. O, I could prophesy,
> But that the earthy and cold hand of death
> Lies on my tongue: no, Percy, thou art dust,
> And food for –
>
> > (V,iv, 76–85)

This speech has an oddly ironic effect. It is the apotheosis of Hotspur; yet simultaneously it is the moment of Hal's greatest triumph. Violence is vindicated at the same time that it produces real tragedy. By virtue of the transmogrifications wrought in drama through deliberately vivid depictions of dying, Hotspur becomes, during this quiet moment in the play, a hero who is the sacrificial creature of his society.[2] The fallen hero speaking and looking upwards at his conqueror commands the world he has lost just as he leaves it; and he does so in a manner and with a completeness that have been denied him up to now. It is the concentration of the audience's, the reader's, the prince's passive energy upon the spectacle of the dying soldier that emphasizes his role as the sacrificial victim of his and our world – a transcendence which involves us with his conqueror and his society in a silent collusion in the sacrifice which has been produced through violence.

Hotspur's death, a palpable and carefully prepared ritual, is directly referable to Prince Hal's vow of fealty to the King, his father.

> Do not think so, you shall not find it so;
> And God forgive them that so much have sway'd
> Your Majesty's good thoughts away from me!
> I will redeem all this on Percy's head,
> And in the closing of some glorious day
> Be bold to tell you that I am your son,
> When I will wear a garment all of blood,
> And stain my favours in a bloody mask,
> Which, wash'd away, shall scour my shame with it;
> And that shall be the day, whene'er it lights,
> That this same child of honour and renown,
> The gallant Hotspur, this all-praised knight,
> And your unthought-of Harry chance to meet.
> For every honour sitting on his helm,
> Would they were multitudes, and on my head
> My shames redoubled! For the time will come
> That I shall make this northern youth exchange
> His glorious deeds for my indignities.
> Percy is but my factor good my lord,
> To engross up glorious deeds on my behalf,
> And I will call him to so strict account
> That he shall render every glory up,
> Yea, even the slightest worship of his time,
> Or I will tear the reckoning from his heart.
> This in the name of God I promise here,
> The which, if He be pleas'd I shall perform,
> I do beseech your Majesty may salve

The long-grown wounds of my intemperance:
If not, the end of life cancels all bands,
And I will die a hundred thousand deaths
Ere break the smallest parcel of this vow.

(III,22,129–59)

The power of the speech derives in part from the solemnity of the vow and its invocation of the imagery of violence and blood sacrifice. Hal's speech is the climax of the play in the sense that the death of Hotspur is given substance and form as an inevitable consequence of what is occurring between the King and the prince.[3] Thus is the destruction of Hotspur by Hal transformed from a shadowy probability into a central fact of the play. It is the fact by which Hotspur becomes the ritual object of a revenger's quest. Resolution through death, as Lawrence Danson argues, 'is necessary to assure the sort of enduring memorial [the hero] and his creator seek, and is an integral part of the play's expressive form'.[4] This shifting emphasis from the probable to the actual takes force less from the known historical details on which the play is based than from the nature of the sacred vow, taken in private and hedged with such images of bloodshed as are traditionally identified with ancient, pre-Christian rites of purification. Such rites, however, are a necessary part of the privileging of violence, of transforming it into an instrument of government.

As the willing captive of drama's most private moments and thus the willing possessor of the secret thoughts and desires of characters in a play, the audience becomes, perforce, a collaborator in the action. That is the mere fact of silent observation of a ceremony (religious, social, theatrical) compels one into a posture of collusion. That the audience is forced to collude in Hal's oath-taking is a consequence of the natural, but nonetheless dramatically contrived, fact of Hotspur's absence which further separates the warrior from the ethical circle of 'right' action to which the audience is a party. The confrontation of father and son, with its ramifying features of paternal accusation leading directly to the solemn blood oath, is a re-enactment of a mythical encounter, a direct step towards purification in a blood ritual through which society itself will be saved, and violence itself consecrated as the necessary tool of authority. The blood images of this speech are unlike almost all the other blood images in the play. Where those elsewhere are emotionally and morally neutral, in Hal's vow, the images of the bloody mask and the garment of blood harness the full force of traditional, even archetypal, mythic sanctity. Hal's promise to redeem himself by shedding Percy's blood is the moment to which the play has logically tended from his first soliloquy – 'I know you all . . . ' – where he promised to reveal his hidden and greater self to the world. In this later private scene, the playwright significantly extends the circle of confidence by one; to the theatre audience is added King Henry himself.[5] In staking his life on his honour, Hal adds potency to his promises by reference to a set of quasi-magical acts and symbols which help to conjure up dire images of fulfilment through the enactment in blood of timeless rites. Such primitive ceremonies inform the conventional concepts of honour and loyalty with new depth and so diverge from the mainstream of acts and images of the drama as to reinforce the idea of Hal's separateness and superiority. Virginia Carr has noted the violations of the cer-emonies of kingship in the Henriad, commencing with Richard II's part in the murder of Thomas Duke of Goucester and reaching their extreme form with the murder of Richard himself in which 'we see the ultimate violation of the sanctity of kingship'.[6] If we accept this view of the causes and manifestations of the destruction of ceremony, we might recognize in Hal's highly ritualized oath and performance of his vow, a gradual, but concrete, reintroduction of the substances and linked ceremonies of kingship into the state and its concomitant absorption of the means of physical control.[7]

It is in distinguishing between beneficial and harmful violence that this drama advances through mime and illusion an age-old practice of blood ritual. Ritual, Rene Girard reminds us, 'is nothing more than the regular exercise of "good" violence'.[8] He adds: 'If sacrificial violence is to be effective it must resemble the non-sacrificial as closely as possible.' Hal's is a promise to commit a deed of 'good' violence, and the elements of ceremony with which he intends to inform the deed only add to its ritualized nature. To Hal, his blood-covered features and the garment of blood are the necessary stage of pollution precedent to the promised regeneration. In these images, Hal imagines himself stained with Hotspur's blood and presenting himself to his father as the conqueror of his father's – and of 'right' society's – enemy, and thus the saviour of the nation. The bloody mask is a token or a ritualistic symbol of his effort on behalf of established order and will publicly proclaim him as hero and publicly demonstrate that the salvation of the nation has been won through the exercise of sanctioned and needed violence. Thus, not only is Hal to be celebrated as a saviour, but also violence itself is mystified as his almost holy means of salvation.

The bloody mask, then possesses great mysterious power, not least as an agent of the valorization of violence as an instrument of social order As a mask it has the power to disguise the wearer. Hal imagines himself not precisely bloody or blood-smeared, but as wearing bloody robes. To *wear* a garment of blood is different from bloodying one's own garments: it can mean to wear outward dress or covering which is stained with blood or to be so covered in blood as to seem to wearing such a robe. The latter reading of this action is used as an assurance of heroic behaviour, as a part of the ritual of purification being described and, furthermore, the latter use accords more literally and immediately with the notion, two lines later, of washing away the accumulated gore on garment and face. The idea of the garment, however, as a separate robe and of the mask as an adopted guise, enforces an impression of Hal as separate from the bloody object, and hence of violence as almost an impersonal social necessity, almost divorced from its controller. In part the self-imagined picture of the prince clad in his garment and mask has the effect of portraying Hal as a priest or ritual slaughterer. As such, the image helps make concrete the early notion, gleaned from Hal's first soliloquy, that Prince Hal is in control of the events of this drama. Seeing himself in the functionary role, Hal is enforcing upon our attention his confident knowledge of himself as director of events. The idea of the garment is more usually associated with the priest's robes than steely armour. The mask, too, is a part of the garb of the priest of common imagination and known tradition who participates in the ritual.

If this is convincing – if Hal's perception of his killing of Hotspur can be accepted as an act of cleansing ('Which washed away shall scour my shame with it') – then we might also accept that Shakespeare has identified yet another crucial, if not *the* crucial difference between the hero and his heroic antagonist. The image of their encounter is variously imagined by Hal and Hotspur, and in this very variety of imagination lies a key to their characters and their different capacities for successful monarchy. Hal shows his own control of his emotions and imagination. As Hotspur can be driven beyond the bounds of patience by imagination of huge exploits, Hal remains firmly anchored within his own sensible sphere. He is the most entirely self-controlled character in the play, perhaps in the canon. In identifying the difference between

Hal and Hotspur, James Calderwood notes that 'as a future king Hal knows very well that his business is to shape history, not be shaped by it. To Hotspur history is a fixed and final reality to which he is irrevocably committed. He has given his word, as it were; he cannot alter his role. To Hal on the other hand history is a series of roles and staged events.'[9]

Hal decidedly lacks what Maynard Mack once characterized as the first quality of the tragic hero – the driving impulse to overstatement[10] – which is possessed in such impressive abundance by Hotspur. For many, Hal seems to have an overdeveloped sense of right and wrong. Equally, and equally unlike Hotspur, part of Hal's amazing political success in the play has to do with his ability to move familiarly through a variety of speech styles and discourses of class and ceremony. We have noted in the speech quoted above the impressive opening line – its straightforwardness, its rhythm, its explicit contrast with the words to which it is a response. Immediately thereafter follow seventeen lines in which Hal commits himself to the fulfillment of a mission through an act of bloodletting. These seventeen lines form a unit which is separate from that dramatic, assertive first line whose loneliness in the speech lends it an air of authenticity of emotion separable from the carefully contrived rhetoric of all that follows. Within the following lines lies deep the notion of vengeance sanitized by reference to the cleansing ritual described. The idea of revenge is concentrated in the imagined destruction of an even greater Hotspur than exists – 'For every honour sitting on his helm, / Would they were multitudes, and on my head / My shames redoubled!' – and is given an even sensual texture by the use and placing of the two key Latinate words in the sentence, 'multitudes' and 'redoubled'. The contrast of these words and this entire section of the speech with the blunt monosyllables of line 1, of the large and conventionally noble concepts of this part of the speech with the sound of outrage and grief conveyed by that first line, lends the speech the tinge of self-consciousness. What follows these seventeen lines seems to me, even more obviously to point to a kind of cleverness in Hal that diminishes the felt rage he is trying to express: for he overlays it with metaphors too mundane to be able to carry the burden of moral distress by which he is ostensibly moved. There is the mercantile terminology by which Hal concludes his plea: 'factor', 'engross up', 'strict account', 'render every glory up', 'tear the reckoning from his heart', 'cancels all bands', 'smallest parcel', establish in the oath-taking a tone of marketplace transaction which stands in contrast with the burnishing imagery of ritual and heroism with which he begins. He introduces here a new mode of speech that contrasts with the heroically extravagant promise of the culminating lines of the preceding part –

> For the time will come
> That I shall make this northern youth exchange
> His glories for my indignities.

Norman Council observes that the speech demonstrates the pragmatic side of the prince who determines here 'to use Hotspur's reputation for his own gain . . . . Hotspur's honorable reputation is useful to Hal and he means to acquire it'.[11] The speech as a whole speaks of the astonishing *competence* of the speaker. The manipulation of styles and the variegation of tones and metaphors all denote a virtuosity which is somewhat vitiated when compared to the different kind of virtuosity of Hotspur's speeches. Finally we might note that the rhetoric of Hal's speech, in all its variety accomplishes its end of gaining the King's good opinion. In this sense, of course, the speech is bound to be suspect, since the whole is motivated by a desire or need to persuade the King, the powerful father, of his loyalty and his capacity to take up arms in the 'legitimate' cause of the monarch and social order. His success and his rhetorical competence are, of course, repaid by the Henry's strong response: 'A hundred thousand rebels die in this.'

All theatre audiences are accustomed to seeing people transformed temporarily into other people for the duration of the play. Audiences and participants in rituals, however, see the process and function of ritual as a means to permanent transformation into, essentially, another person. Through rituals a boy becomes a man, a girl a woman, a man a priest. Most Shakespeare critics have been united in recognizing the transformation of Hal from wayward boyhood to manhood after this speech to his father. Harold Jenkins, for example, sees this exchange between father and son as the 'nodal point' of the play.[12] One may go further, I believe, in recognizing the transformation of the protagonist of the play into a hero – and one may identify the moment of transformation as the first line of this speech. To recognize the transformation as made permanent by virtue of a ritualized oathtaking founded on a violent act has the effect of strengthening and universalizing the nature and extent of the change and, hence, of adumbrating with certainty the triumph of this hero in a drama which seems to depend frequently upon the formal modes of myth.

I say 'this hero' because the uniqueness of *1 Henry IV* resides very largely in the fact that this is a play with two heroes, each of whom stands at the centre of a world which has been conceived in opposition to that of the other. Those worlds are separately defined units of place and ideology which cannot coexist; for their separate existences are partially defined by the pledge of each to destroy the other. The ideologies for which the two heroes stand are at bottom the same – power, patriarchy, and control of the instruments of violence.

The encounter between them is the occasion of the play's greatest emotional intensity. The moment has been predicted, vaunted, hoped for by the participants and the heroes themselves. The privacy of the confrontation – interrupted briefly by Douglas and Falstaff – does not in any sense diminish the force of the timeless ritual with which it is informed. We note the common expressions of recognition and identification, whose tone of defiance maintains the note of hostility necessary to such life-and-death meetings as these. And we note the nearly compulsive need of each hero to articulate to the other his sense of the meaning of the moment. The form of the expression of each is remarkable: Hal's chivalry and Hotspur's haste are appropriate symbolic denotions of each as he is given the opportunity to express his sense of the significance of the moment, demonstrating that he knows, as his opposite knows, that for one of them it is a last encounter. It is this awareness of finality that endues the moment with solemnity and the ritual with its form – that of a last accounting, in the dazzling light of a certain death to follow.

The encounter, when it finally comes, is preceded by a provocative ritual of boasting in which each of the combatants – almost as if to recover the basis of his hatred of the other – recalls the very spirit of his own animosity. In Hal's recollection of the Ptolemaic principle that 'Two stars keep not their motion in one sphere' he falls back upon the natural law, resistance to which he has begun to abandon since his vow to the King. And indeed it is in obedience to the ideologically charged laws of nature that Hal has ritually dedicated himself. Hotspur's overweening vanity makes him hark back, compulsively almost, to the lust for greatness that dooms him. But it is when Hal, oddly and mockingly, borrows Hotspur's own demotic language and metaphors of violent action, that the Northern youth is finally left almost wordless with violent fury and must strike:

> *Prince.* I'll make it greater ere I part from thee
> And all the budding honours on thy crest
> I'll crop to make a garland for my head.
> *Hotspur.* I can no longer brook thy vanities.
>
> (V,iv,70–3)

Hal's confident words, his image of Hotspur's 'budding' honours, suggest to his adversary that those honours are not yet full-grown, not really the honours of an adult. His threat to 'crop' them from his crest contains an insulting contempt. The word carries the easy arrogance of a simple, almost casual, single deadly blow. In Hal's brilliantly infuriating image we and, more important, Hotspur are presented with the image of Hotspur as an unresisting plant and the prince as a carefree courtier in search of a garland. Hotspur's single line of reply is reasonably one of powerful anger: his only possible reply to Hal's 'vanities' is the testing action of combat.

Of the dying Hotspur, George Hibbard has written that he 'eventually becomes capable of seeing all human endeavour, including his own, in relation to the great abstract ideas of time and eternity, and voices this vision of things in the moving lines he utters at the end'.[13] This insight helps to explain the tragic element of this character in the coalescence of his comic and tragic selves into mutually supporting images of comedy and tragedy whose very extremism lends intensity to the character. There is tragedy in the dying man's magnificent self honesty, his truth to what he is and has been;

> I better brook the loss of brittle life
> Than those proud titles thou has won of me

comes not from the large heart of the tragedy but from the authentic, single, separate self of Harry Hotspur, uniquely and eternally apart. That difference from his fellows, from all other heroes, is gloriously captured in the penultimate realization that the instrument by which he has lived, by which his life and character have been defined, has been stilled – 'the cold hand of death / Lies on my tongue'. Hotspur, whose eloquence has elevated him, is unimaginable in a silent state, and so we are directed to the death of his speech as his tragedy. With the death of Hotspur comes, for a moment, the end of rebellion and 'bad' violence. Yet the informing tragedy of the death of Hotspur spontaneously reconfirms the play's complex construction of the issue of violence. The triumph of 'good' violence that the defeat of Hotspur implies is subverted by the fact that it is Hotspur himself who has been felled. And no amount of rationalization about the social necessity of Hotspur's death removes the sense of tragic loss that it supplies.

The prolonged antagonism of Hal and Hotspur has no obviously alternative outcome to this final violent conflict. And in the conflict itself we can discern the fact that the physical closeness of the antagonists is a metaphor for a larger issue evident in the spectacle: that as the two have been driven gradually closer through the play, so have they become with the subtle aid of ritual more and more alike until, in the moments of and after the fatal fight, they appear almost as images of each other. During fights differences between combatants tend to disappear: the violence is the correlative by which individuals are connected as their whole selves are absorbed by physical contention. Hal and Hotspur do not speak during their fight; they are transformed by their attempts to kill each other into a single unit of dramatic action – the differences between them disappear, their personalities seem to meld into the thing they have become as they become one. The text itself proposes that in killing Hotspur Hal has absorbed something of his being or essence.

His farewell to Hotspur takes the form of a ritualized tribute to a fallen hero. Herbert Hartmann has argued that as he says the words, Hal disengages his own royal plumes from his helmet to shroud the face of his dead rival.[14] These plumes are equivalent to Hotspur's 'budding honours' and thus Hal's act of placing them upon the face of his former enemy is a gesture of weight. In the purest sense of the phrase, Hal *identifies with* Hotspur, and that identification is given a poignant depth by the ritualistic means through which it is achieved. In addition, by himself finishing Hotspur's dying speech, Hal has appropriated something of his rival's speech; he has almost literally absorbed his last breath. Despite the obviousness of the tendency of Hotspur's last words, Hal's capacity to utter these words – 'For worms' – cements the identification. The scene here is a significant valorization of violence. It is through bloodshed that Hal can fulfil the demands made upon authority. He has not just proven himself strongest. He has done so by strongly indicating the relationship between his physical skill and strength and his willingness to serve the embedded structure of power. The ritualistic emblems and actions of this scene and the oath scene have strengthened the connection.

Ten lines later, concomitantly with his 'rites of tenderness', Prince

Hal bends over the body of Hotspur to lay his favours on the warrior's face. In so doing he once again closes the physical space between them as he touches his former adversary. Hal thus bathes his own favours in Hotspur's blood. And thus, ironically, does Hotspur acquire a mask soaked in his own blood *and* the blood of the prince. For, as Hal performs the act of homage, we are reminded of his oath to the King to 'stain my favours in a bloody mask'. In the mingling of the blood of Prince Hal and Harry Hotspur is the fusion of the two symbolically extended. The words by which Hal accompanies his gesture complete the connection: 'And even in thy behalf I'll thank myself . . . ' (V, iv, 96). The pronouns of that line bind their subjects more firmly to each other by their self-conscious interplay. As well, history furnished Shakespeare with an additional means by which the two characters are made to merge; that is of course the fact that they have the same first name.

The degradation of honour and courage which Falstaff's presence offers the scene has been discussed frequently. Falstaff's brutal defilement of the body that lay near him is an example of violence that is unritualized, illegitimate, and unsanctioned by the rage for the 'social good' that characterizes the fight just witnessed. As such it is presented and perceived as mere brutality. The action is placed in a precise relation to the Prince's killing of Hotspur. A nation in a state of civil war is one in which law has failed to create or maintain order. And so it is beyond the law that the state must seek the means of stability. The means are often those of repression, which always carry and imply the threat of resistance. Thus the two opposing forces of tyranny and resistance promise the fruition of actual conflict. Societies suffering repression can explode in violence. As the violent riots of *Henry VI* are shown to issue from and result in criminal disorder, in 1 *Henry IV* the conflict and its hero are presented so as to emphasize a socially beneficial outcome. Here the blood that is shed fulfills the requirements of blood rituals. It is, one might say, 'clean' blood, resulting from what Girard has called 'good' violence.[15] That is, it is blood which has been shed for the larger advantage of the nation as a whole. And as we look back at the blood imagery related to the Hal/Hotspur conflict, it becomes clear that Hotspur's blood has been represented as that of the sacrificial creature whose death will redeem his world, and into whose life and persona are concentrated the rage, anxiety, and fear of a threatened nation. His death, then, sometimes regarded as tragic, is also represented in this monarchical ideology as necessary for the continuation of the nation. Dover Wilson regards it as a favourable feature of Hal's character that his 'epitaph on Hotspur contains not a word of triumph'.[16] For Shakespeare's audiences, however, more significant may be the fact that Hotspur's vaunted greatness was very nearly sufficient to his purposes: the world was almost overturned, and with it the reign of the regicide Henry IV.

At his death and because of it, Hotspur is transformed into a hero of tragic magnitude. Thus, when Falstaff rises and hacks at his corpse, he commits a direct assault on the sanctity of the ritual that has just taken place. His act suddenly infuses the scene with uncleanness by an almost casual reversal of the ritual that has been solemnly performed. The return to life of Falstaff is no miracle but a rather sour joke. The return to prose, to a deliberately disordered and unrhythmic speech which breathes selfish relief and opportunism is a vicious riposte to Hal. But the physical attack on Hotspur's corpse is a kind of deliberate crime against the ethos of heroism and 'good' violence to which the prince and the nation (in the person of the king) have been committed. Falstaff's act is a negation and a degradation of the cleansing by blood. And yet the repeated exposure to violence can inure us to it. While we might be shocked by the callous treatment of Hotpur's corpse, the very brutality of that treatment and its extensiveness gradually accustom us to the initially shocking fact that a slain hero is being dragged around like a side of beef. Hotspur's corpse gradually becomes the focus of a grotesque successful joke – 'one of the best jokes in the whole drama'[17] – upon whose point is balanced the question of ritual purification. Yet Falstaff's imitative act of violence rebounds upon himself: any doubts as to his locus in the moral scheme of the play are vividly resolved by his disruption of the cycle of the ritual. That is, he is expelled from the circle of power and 'beneficial' violence. The emphatic terminus implied by Hal's parting words is crassly mocked by Falstaff rising up. The act of cutting Percy's thigh is represented as antithetical to Hal's death-fight with Percy: as the fight was a lucid example of the purifying violence seen only in drama and ritual, so the attack on the corpse affirmed the value of the rite by its implied but debased re-enactment of the encounter.

Hal, Hotspur, and Falstaff are, then, related through a ritual of violence, a ritual which exists on its own and through the dark glass of parody and travesty. Furthermore, it is through this ritual that they are connected to their world in the play's intensest moments. To call Falstaff's impersonation of Hal's father in the tavern scene a parody is to diminish the force of a scene in which a youth enacts one of the deepest universal desires of man as he overthrows his tyrannical father. The scene of oathtaking, discussed above, is a conscious, deliberate, and calculated retraction of the desires enacted in the tavern. As such, it is either utterly false or it is the heroic conquest of reason and responsibility – i.e. social pressure and expectation – over the urging of the unconscious mind – i.e. individual nature. It is thus profitable to see the tavern ritual and its climactic, if soft-spoken, conclusion ('I do, I will') as a ritual of exorcism by which Prince Hal, through the contrived dramatization of his innermost promptings, rids himself of the demons of his deepest desires. As. J. I. M. Stewart has argued with reference to the rejection of Falstaff: Hal, 'by a displacement common enough in the evolution of a ritual, kills Falstaff instead of killing the king, his father'.[18]

Hotspur, on the other hand, does not grow or change, From first to last his purpose is to gain glory and renown. Even at his death, it is to his honours that he refers as having been more dearly won of him than his life. His obdurate consistency makes him an apt victim in the cruel drama of ritual sacrifice by which he becomes a means for the social and moral cleansing of his vanquisher. A Hotspur who can go to his death proclaiming the value of a moral system which is by its nature exclusive of the vast world from which it derives, cannot be the hero who heals the world. His presence nearly always provides discordancy. He is the heart of the whirlwind that rages through the nation, and it is this heart that must be stilled for the sake of what the court calls peace. As with other tragic characters, Hotspur's death is the necessary means for recovering a form of order that ensures the continuity on which the monarch and his son stake their lives.

4

The Culture of Violence
in 2 *Henry IV*

The schism between prose and verse plots in 2 *Henry IV* is an index
of the political dimension of the play's manifestation as an instrument of the patriarchal system which produced it. In recognizing the
function of the differentiation between these plots we come closer to
understanding one of the ways in which the concept of ideology is
deployed by tracing the 'cultural connections between signification
and legitimation'.[1] Wittingly or not and ambiguously or not, by its
very existence the play is a piece of direct propaganda that serves
the interests of the dominant class of the social formation from
which it issues. Its use in the centuries since it was first written and
produced testifies to the overwhelming capacity of the societies it
has served to incorporate, absorb, and appropriate the results of the
individual and collective labours of their members. The distinction
within the play between its disparate worlds of comedy and court
has usually been made to support the patriarchal value systems of
the societies in which it is produced and taught. David Margolies
notes that the force of the hegemonic use of Shakespeare lies 'in the
use of the plays as a whole, in how they have been 'naturalised'
into the dominant ideology'.[2] While it is true that some of the most
adversarial and critical political points are made in the vernacular
by ordinary characters, it is also true, as Margot Heinemann asserts,
that the ruling class maintains its commercial and ideological hold
on the play in production by routinely presenting these 'low' characters as 'gross, stupid and barely human – rogues, sluts and varlets
with straw in their hair, whose antics the audience can laugh at but
whose comments it can't be expected to take seriously. Indeed, the
combination of Loamshire dialect and dated jokes often makes the
comments unintelligible anyway'.[3]

The political and dramatic value of Eastcheap is an established feature of the criticism of the play. Eastcheap travesties Westminster; it inverts it and thus provides one of the potential displacements of that dominant political world. It fleshes out the England of the play and shows that England's ordinary people, like its high people, have hearts, souls, and minds. Eastcheap, however, is not only a funny place, a locus of irresponsibility and mirth: it is also an ugly place of violence and poverty and corruption. And it is these aspects of the play which I wish to address. I believe that most discussions of the 'low' comedy of the play are presented and analysed conservatively. That is, the dominant responses to the 'low' comedy of the play have been largely determined by what Greenblatt has called the 'monological' approach of scholarship which is itself an example of the readings it has recovered from the play.[4] The 'low' comedy of *2 Henry IV* has been used both on stage and in criticism to support the hierarchical and patriarchal structures that produced the play and which criticism avers dominates it. The most influential such analysis is, probably, Dover Wilson's *The Fortunes of Falstaff*,[5] whose exculpation of Prince Hal still forms the basis of most such arguments. It is widely accepted that the scenes of prose comedy provide an alternative action to the court scenes. That is, the prose comic scenes are directly linked, by parody and symbiosis, to those verse scenes of high seriousness. Neither world exists independently of the other. The court needs the comedy to give it humanity and to expose it. The comedy needs the court to give itself something to parody. These mutual needs, however, go deeper than those of mere theatricality. Power structures always exist in vertical relationships. The court, in other words, needs the comedy so that it can be the court. Comedy – virtually synonymous with poverty in the play – needs the court so that it can exist as comedy.

In *2 Henry IV* the links between the court and the tavern are far less a part of the author's design of a unified world than much traditional reading has taught us to believe. The essential point about the comedy of this play is that it represents a world which is incompatible with and separate from the world of political power. The agents of political power are violence and repression; these are the instruments by which power contains the disaffection of the poor and their impulses of subversion within a vertical structure of material wellbeing in which they are at the bottom. The deeper we get into that comic world – the more complex and intricate its relationships seem, the more solid its traditions, lore, and mysteries – the more complete we discover its separateness from the 'serious' world to be. This is not to discount or challenge the critical notion of the interrelatedness of the various plots. Rather, I wish to propose that the relationship of the plots in the play is as tentative and contingent as the 'low' characters perceive their relationship to the world of power to be, and that the severance of the worlds of poverty and power is deliberately maintained and encouraged by the world of power. Power has manipulated poverty into intensifying the separateness by creating conditions in the world of poverty which demand the development of social and political practices ultimately under its (power's) own control.

Notwithstanding its complexity, the prose of *2 Henry IV* is an evident means of deepening the division between power and poverty. Brian Vickers has demonstrated that the prose has the effect of 'conveying information about particular characters who are below the dignity and norm of verse'.[6] The worlds of prose and verse meet rarely in the play, but when they do meet, as in the rejection scene, for example, the meeting is a violent collision in which prose is discomfited. A revealing encounter of this kind is, for example, the occasion in Part I at Shrewsbury when Falstaff dares to interject during the hard and charged verse dialogue between Worcester and the king:

> *Worcester.*   Hear me my liege.
> For mine own part, I could be well content
> To entertain the lag-end of my life
> With quiet hours, for I protest
> I have not sought the day of this dislike.
> > *King.*   You have not sought it? How comes it then?
> > *Falstaff.*   Rebellion lay in his way, and he found it.
> > *Prince.*   Peace, chewet, peace!
>
> > (V, i, 22–9)

Falstaff's interruption and Hal's reaction introduce a social complication. The smoothly functioning dialogue is disrupted by an intrusive sarcasm that wittily calls into question the entire structure of authority implied in the exchange. Falstaff interrupts the king; interposing himself between Worcester and Henry, he supplies an impudent answer for Worcester and, in so doing, mocks both the rebellion and the monarchy by subverting the high solemnity of the moment. Hal's reaction, embarrassed or angry, is designed to put an end to the disruption, to enable monarchy and support established authority. And, of course, it succeeds. Falstaff doesn't open his mouth again until the king and Worcester are gone.

The comedy of Part 2 begins with Falstaff trying to penetrate the ranks of power. His cynicism and open avarice, expressed most notoriously in his determination to 'turn diseases into commodity' (I,i,250), have been the delight of some critics who have recognized a virtue in his frankness – a contrast, they say, to the hypocrisy of the court. The celebration of Falstaff's candour has itself served the forces of established order under the terms of that celebration. That order has developed sufficient resilience over the centuries to be able to absorb an amount of self-criticism and, even, subversion as long as it is not endangered. The criticism that can valorize Falstaff, can do so only in terms that are themselves absorbable by the social order. Falstaff is, after all defeated, his ambitions are alternatively constructable as delusions. For all its subversive possibilities, the narrative impulses of the play destroy him and the political, judicial, social, psychological, and economic upheaval adumbrated in his potential triumph. It seems to me erroneous to argue, however, that the play offers the vision of Falstaff's rule in its alternatively depicted actions or in Falstaff's megalomaniacal fantasies. When he proposes to ennoble Shallow or to take any man's horses, or when he declares that the laws of England are at his commandment, he only proposes one vision of his rule. But it is at moments like these that the drama becomes an overtly political instrument; Falstaff's declarations grossly reify the established order. His dramatic func-tion becomes circumscribed by being contained within the limits of an antithesis already well established in the play – his own, for example, to the Lord Chief Justice. Some may laugh at the idea of the reign of Falstaff, some may be horrified by it. Some may argue that the idea offers a world that is very little different from that which presently exists. The point is that what is offered by way of alternative – and alternatives do abound, not least in the king's proleptic description of chaos – is always partial, and always produced in the play in terms of static and hierarchical values. By way of egregious example: no-one in the play puts into words the idea that the monarchy may be overthrown and replaced by a non-hierarchical communism. That alternative is imaginable, perhaps, but it has no perceptible touchstones within the dialogue of the play nor are there appropriate historical referents to give it imaginative reality. As an option it could exist only in the minds of certain readers.

The much-quoted alternative to the rule of order is the speech of
the king to Hal in IV, v:

> Harry the fifth is crown'd! Up vanity!
> Down, royal state! All you sage counsellors, hence!
> And to the English court assemble now
> From every region, apes of idleness!
> Now, neighbour confines, purge you of your scum!
> Have you a ruffian that will swear, drink, dance,
> Revel the night, rob, murder, and commit
> The oldest sins the newest kind of ways?
> Be happy, he will trouble you no more.
> England shall double gild his treble guilt,
> England shall give him office, honour, might:
> For the fifth Harry from curb'd license plucks
> The muzzle of restraint, and the wild dog
> Shall flesh his tooth on every innocent.
>
>   (120–32)

The rule of Hal promises to be different from the present rule, and
it is clear that he will have to make the choice of following in his
father's footsteps or creating a new direction for the nation. But the
construction of disorder is merely one of the play's many images of
moral chaos designed to serve the entrenched structure of authority.
For its images are all contingent on the rule of crime and criminals,
on a vision of the nation as a wilderness of savage dogs, riot, sin,
foreign scum, and ruffians dancing and drinking in the street. This
notion of a nation governed by moral madmen is political and
rhetorical, though it refers to a frequently expressed fear by 'those in
charge of Elizabethan and Jacobean England that disaffection might
escalate into organized resistance'.[7] It really proposes government
by the poor as they are represented in the play. Henry's view of
the tavern is a characteristic demonization, within the echelons of
the privileged, of the forces of potential subversion. It is a typical
example of the ideological displacement of the disorder generated
by his rule onto those who are least politically powerful in his
kingdom and therefore most vulnerable to such displacement. C.
L. Barber has made the point that such inversions as the linguistic,
in which Carnival is put on trial, are malign *demonstrations* of the
potential destruction of society.[8] The king warns the prince against
the people with whom he has been associating, and does so in terms

designed to represent their worthlessness. If this vision has validity, then where does it leave Eastcheap? And what is 'Eastcheap'?

The prince, of course, makes his choice to support monarchy and the traditions of his father in words that make plain his commitment to the conservative political values of patriarchy and order. In his most ceremonially solemn moments in the play he alludes directly to the tradition, to the values of his father, and to his determination to continue them:

> Not Amurath an Amurath succeeds,
> But Harry Harry.
>
> (V,ii,48–9)

And to the Lord Chief Justice:

> And I do wish your honours may increase
> Till you do live to see a son of mine
> Offend you and obey you, as I did.
> So shall I live to speak my father's words.
>
> (105–8)

Hal's words are a repudiation of Eastcheap and Eastcheap values. And if audiences and readers have been relieved at his recovery it is no wonder. For the play has made havoc of its own underworld. Notwithstanding its occasional subversive celebration of the mirth and pleasure in the stews, it is unambiguous about the calamitous political morality that obtains there. It is simply not a viable alternative to the rule of Henry. The rebels, on the other hand, with their political and military power are a real threat to the king's position. But the threat is contemplated without horror. The potential rule of the rebels is not a rule of chaos, of nightmarish inversion. It is clearly understood by Henry's party that the rule of the rebels would be a substitutive rule. As Elliot Krieger has noted with regard to Part 1, 'The rebel forces . . . oppose the state (not just as represented by King Henry; they want to divide the kingdom itself among themselves) without opposing the principle of authority.'[9] Speaking the same language as the present monarchy, their rule promises to maintain the structure of hierarchical values already in place. The classes, under the rebels, would remain divided – prose and verse divisions ensure that. The threat of Eastcheap, on the other hand, is a threat to the entire system of classification.

Now the king, the prophet of national doom, never sees
Eastcheap. In common, I believe, with most of the audiences and
readers of Shakespeare in the last two or three centuries, his view of
tavern life and poverty is largely imaginary and literary. The separation from that world is important. This is not to say that he is wrong
– or right – about that world. Rather it is to recall that his separation
from it releases him from the responsibility entailed in knowing; it
releases his imagination. Eastcheap is indeed another 'world', and
not just in the dramatic sense. And its different language is merely
one of the features of that otherness. In his discussion of *Measure for
Measure*, Jonathan Goldberg makes the point that everyone in that
play arrives in the prison 'so that it reconstitutes the world and
erases the margin between the world outside the prison walls'.[10]
Prince Hal is often thought of as the means of linking the two worlds
of *Henry IV*, or erasing the margins between them. However, there
really is no such erasure in *2 Henry IV*, no such intermingling in the
play. Prince Hal's command of tavern language – in Part One he
boasts, 'I can drink with any tinker in his own language' (II,iv,20)
– powerfully maintains the structure of separations necessary to the
relation of power and powerlessness.

The first scene to be specifically set in Eastcheap begins with
Hostess Quickly and Fang and Snare employed to arrest Falstaff
for debt. Snare is afraid of Falstaff, 'for he will stab' (II,i,11). The
fear gives rise to one of the play's better-known *double-entendres* as
the Hostess declares:

> Alas the day, take heed of him – he stabbed me in mine
> own house, most beastly in good faith. A cares not
> what mischief he does, if his weapon be out; he will
> foin like any devil, he will spare neither man, woman,
> nor child.
>
> (II,i,13–17)

Aside from the fact of this speech being in prose, there are elements
of it that mark the class of its speaker and the world from which
it issues. While it is certainly true that some of the most glowing
Shakespearean heroines engage in bawdy talk without damaging
their reputations or losing their status, there remains a significant difference between the present example of bawdiness and
those other. First of all on the level of sheer consciousness: when
Desdemona, Rosalind, or Portia use bawdy conversation, they do

so with wit and full awareness of the meaning of what they are saying. The notable – and funny – thing about Hostess Quickly's speech is that she seems not to understand what she means. As far as I know there is no way of knowing what she knows except under the manipulation of an actor or director. Can it be that she thinks that Snare's fear of Falstaff is sexual? If so, the implications of her speech become outrageous and illogical. If, on the other hand, she understands Snare as we understand him; that Falstaff's propensity to stab people with knives and swords frightens him, then her speech becomes outrageous in another way. She says that he stabbed her in her own house, and she means, if she is confirming Snare's reasonable fear of being knifed, that he stuck a knife or dagger into her flesh. And we laugh. Naturally, we have to laugh because the text is formally made funny at that moment by the palpable use of sexual equivocation.

The equivocation, however, is subtextual. It depends on external recognition. And it has been put there by a very clever man. For the equivocation lends an enormous authority to the laughers. Their (our) laughter is a declaration of the willingness to accept the fusion of violence with sexuality and stupidity in the world of Eastcheap. The laughter depends upon a subtextual, shared recognition within the audience or among readers. The hostess's words, we are made to see, contradict themselves in a curious way. We note the contradiction and we laugh at her, in part, because she does not note it. But nor do Fang or Snare note the contradiction. They, after all, are part of this world of lawlessness and fear. The subtlety of the joke, the dependency on the recognition of wit by those outside the play, and the failure of such recognition by those within it, who – unlike us – are too stupid to understand it, have the simple effect of deepening the division between the two worlds within the play and of placing the audience in an alliance with the mirthless world of the court and power.

The humour is given shape as Falstaff enters and a violent altercation occurs. Falstaff's fearsome rage and violent threats – 'Draw Bardolph! Cut me off the villain's head! Throw the quean into the channel!' (45–6) – have the wild farcical force of comic cartoons. They, and the actions that surround them – noisy, confused, chaotic – propose the possibility of violence without making it a likely outcome. The risibility of this episode, unlike that of the passage of *double entendre*, comes from the fact that a harmless outcome stands as one of its immediate and initial conditions. This is achieved by the use of outrageous exaggeration of implied gesture and language, and reasonable audience expectation of the shape of the future.

It is interesting, nevertheless, to note how the violence is put to an end and order is restored. The Lord Chief Justice and his men intrude into the scene of violence. The forces of order and power arrive and demonstrate, once again, their capacity to contain riot and murder. However, the effect of this recovery has at least two significant social by-products. One is to reassert the value of patriarchy and hierarchy – society needs to have the instruments of physical suppression at its command. The other by-product of the intervention at this threatening moment is to contain poverty. Eastcheap, bursting with potential violence and the threat, therefore, of serious social disruption, needs to be accessible to authority. It is a fact that the prince and the Lord Chief Justice can enter Eastcheap at will; the reverse situation is obviously not true. The inhabitants of this ghetto are utterly excluded from the world of authority. We have seen, for example, one instance where Falstaff – who occupies an ambiguous lower-middle ground between Eastcheap and the court – is chastised for not following the rules of court. The rejection scene makes even clearer the need to follow the rules.

The court's existence is contingent. It needs to keep the military power to maintain that existence and it needs to maintain the illusion of its own social necessity. The people need to believe that it is mighty and necessary for their own sakes. The existence of Eastcheap is contingent under entirely other conditions. But the overriding condition of its continued existence is that it be ultimately subject to the court. What happens in Eastcheap, we note, is of little concern to the court except insofar as it concerns the prince. The talk of violence, dishonesty and deception is personal, casual and everyday. These are conditions of life in the world of the poor. And, for the most part, they go on until they interrupt the workings of the state – in this case by involving the prince. The condition of visibility is crucial. Eastcheap needs to be identifiable to authority so that its power structures can be contained. In the play that visibility is maintained by a multiplicity of systems and social and psychological structures.

One psychological structure is the motive of social formation, the urge to be part of a structure. That is, the material conditions of the divided worlds of wealth and poverty compel community. It is unnecessarily paranoic to regard this spontaneous community of poverty as part of a conspiracy of power over poverty, but we ought not overlook the way in which this tendency to form groups is made to serve the system of power. The important question of why, and under what conditions differentiated collectivities of people come to be organized in terms of one ideology rather than another is produced by the powerful/powerless dichotomy of the play and represented by its clearly marked patterns of differentiation such as, for example, its linguistic and discursive forms. Power tends to surround, locate, and determine powerlessness. We might note that in 2 *Henry IV* authority can invade, defeat, and contain Eastcheap at will. The ease with which this can be managed is shown in the effect of the Lord Chief Justice's intrusion. He brings order and submission back to Eastcheap, and, notwithstanding Falstaff's verbal fencing with him in this scene, the Lord Chief Justice's last words – 'Now the Lord lighten thee, thou art a great fool' (190) – make very clear his authority over this world to which he doesn't quite belong.

Language and place help to isolate poverty – they make it recognizable and they keep it contained. Language, as I have proposed, functions in part to make poverty comic. It also has the power to make physical violence comic. The farcical momentum of violence in the first Eastcheap scene acquires new impetus in the major tavern scene of the play – Act II, scene iv. As a whole this play has an overriding political force which is designed not just to marginalize Falstaff, but to contain and separate the whole of Eastcheap. The value of separation as an instrument of political control is largely contingent on the presentation of physical violence in Eastcheap. Greenblatt's argument and demonstration that in Renaissance culture 'contemporary authorities tried to contain or, when containment seemed impossible, to destroy' subversion is validated by the representations of the relations between authority and Eastcheap.[11] Greenblatt's point is that power produces subversion as part of the process of containment: and, indeed, Eastcheap, and the form which it takes, are inevitable products of the process of containment. In this scene the effects of violence, from the point of view of the narrative, remain farcical largely by the ironically neutralizing use of sexual innuendo. While physical harm is really possible on one level, on another that possibility is effaced by the deflection of that threat. If a sword or dagger is constructed as a phallus, and rape a tavern joke (significantly, it is *never* a court joke), the idea of an attack with a sword is automatically split into two possibilities – one harmful and one harmless, one serious and one comic. The immediate and automatic association of the contradictory possibilities vitiates or neutralizes the danger.

Pistol, whose entrance arouses passionate responses, is the source of much violent language in this scene. His offer to 'charge' (119) Doll Tearsheet elicits a vicious harangue and Doll's warning: 'I'll thrust my knife in your mouldy chaps and you play the saucy cuttle with me' (126–7). This sentence, in the middle of a speech of comic invective is unequivocal and therefore unfunny. It alerts us to the habit of violence in Eastcheap and to its real potential for social harm.

Eastcheap has two languages of violence. The equivocal language of violence where violent bodily harm is made equivalent to and synonymous with the sexual act is one kind of language where the real potential for harm and danger is neutralized by a sexual meaning. Then there is the direct language of violence, unambiguous, deliberate, precise. 'I'll thrust my knife in your mouldy chaps' is uncomic largely because of its use of detail, and precision. It is the kind of language that uses some of the devices of realism – especially local specificity – for its effect. It operates without subtextual or comic meaning and thus makes the threat it proposes the more real seeming.

Hal and Poins eavesdrop on Falstaff boasting to Doll Tearsheet. Their asides to each other, as they allow Falstaff to continue bragging, exemplify this kind of direct and undisguised language of violence found in Eastcheap:

> *Prince.*   Would not this nave of wheel have his ears cut off?
> *Poins.*   Let's beat him before his whore.
>
> (253–5)

Hal's threat is somewhat abstract and speculative, expressive of nothing so much as his anger and a quasi-comic wish for an extravagant punishment for the treacherous old villain. Poins, however, has a real and available resolution: to beat Falstaff and then to compound the 'humiliation' of the beating by doing it before 'his whore'. The conjunction of the two punishments argue a structure of violence that is almost ritualized by repetition. Poins proposes to inflict physical suffering and public shame as a way of teaching Falstaff a lesson. It is as though he is arguing the social efficacy of this form of violence. The precision of the violence of such lines, which occur only in the prose scenes of the play, is what makes them seem real and more horrible than the grandiosity of the violent language in the court scenes. When, in Part One, for example, Hal promises to kill Hotspur, he tells the king that he will wear a garment all of blood, that he will stain his favours in a bloody mask. He tells Hotspur at the moment of encounter not that he intends to shove a sword into his guts, but, rather, that he will crop Hotspur's honours to wear as a garland. The difference between Poins and Hal, indicated by their remarks as they eavesdrop, signifies a difference in their classes, in the worlds to which they really belong. Hal's words denote control through hyperbole – no-one thinks he intends to cut off Falstaff's ears. Poins, on the other hand, speaks of a violent retribution that has real potential expression in the context of the scene. His threat, in a way, is almost reasonable and precedented. He belongs to this world of vice and prose and his knowledge of such punishments as beating Falstaff before his whore brings the ugliness of the prospect unpleasantly close.[12]

In Part Two, the notorious threat of violence in the verse scenes of the play is Northumberland's invocation of a spirit of universal bloodshed:

> Let order die!
> And let this world no longer be a stage to feed
> contention in a ling'ring act;
> But let one spirit of the first-born Cain
> Reign in all bosoms, that, each heart being set
> On bloody courses, the rude scene may end,
> And darkness be the burier of the dead!
>
> (I,i,154–60)

There is no question about the passion for violence and vengeance expressed in these words. Northumberland is revealing his capability, even his desire, to stick knives and swords into other people's bodies, to cut off their heads and throw them into the channel. But such details are not provided at times or in places like these. This is the world of the court, of real power, of potential monarchy, and the illusion of government and self-government must be maintained. Grim though Northumberland's vision of violent retribution may be, more sickening by far is the idea of Tearsheet's knife in Pistol's chaps. The antithesis of order in Northumberland's construction is freedom to commit murder. Order, that is, stands as political control.

It is going too far to suggest that the violence of the court is presented in a sanitized form, though it is normally justified in terms of its political and social value. Thus when Northumberland's friends protest at his 'strained passion' (I,i,161) they are protesting at the way his call for destruction robs their enterprise of social and political value and validity. Northumberland's world of destruction greatly resembles the king's vision of the rule of ruffianism. All verse speakers agree – with the temporary exception of the grieving father, Northumberland – that the tavern and its inhabitants, the poor of the play, must be kept separate from the court. The distinctions of class must be maintained for the world to be governable. The poor must contained and controlled. Even a rebel government would be preferable to a social revolution. The ideology of order espoused by the rebels shows their desire to continue the hierarchical and patriarchal political practice already in place. The only true opposition to this order is in the riotous and violent tavern. The rural poor that we see are disunited and utterly obedient to authority, to the very point of approving its function, as Feeble's famous patriotic utterance eloquently shows.

Murder, obliquely referred to in Northumberland's summons of the spirit of Cain, truly exists only in the tavern. In Act V, scene iv, the beadles have come to arrest Doll Tearsheet and Hostess Quickly for murder. The First Beadle mentions the murder in the same breath as a joke about false pregnancy:

> *Hostess.*   O the Lord, that Sir John were come! He
> would make this a bloody day to somebody. But I
> pray God the fruit of her womb miscarry!
> *First Beadle.* If it do, you shall have a dozen of
> cushions again; you have but eleven now. Come I
> charge you both, go with me, for the man is dead
> that you and Pistol beat amongst you.

$$(12–18)$$

This is chilling. These characters we have been prepared to laugh at have really meant what they have been saying all along. They really do kill people. Stabbing and cutting off heads has ceased to be the jokey hyperbole of the early scenes, and the need to contain poverty and its ugly consequences is made more urgent.

This murdering by beating touches us more nearly than the large mythologies encompassed in the Northumberland curse: a man has been beaten to death by two characters who possess more humanity, ordinariness, and recognizable frailty than all the kings, princes, and earls of the cycle.[13]

The need for the containment of this potential violence at our doorsteps is fulfilled theatrically. From this world of murder and crime we are removed to a world of stability and certainty. Ritual and order are restored with the entrance of grooms announcing the time of day accompanied by the sounds of ceremony. Trumpets blare, and the new king passes over the stage. His appearance is a reminder of the power he embodies. His train includes those characters who determine the directions of the nation, enforce its laws, hold its security in their hands: the Lord Chief Justice is with him, so is his brother John. The presence of the latter and his ready embrace by Hal confirms Greenblatt's claim that the moral authority of monarchical power in England 'rests upon a hypocrisy so deep that the hypocrites themselves believe it.'[14]

King Henry V passes over the stage surrounded by the agents of political control. The stage is then given to Falstaff, the very man Hostess Quickly is relying on to rescue her from a charge of murder which she hasn't even bothered to deny. As King Hal returns, Falstaff, who seems virtually to have exploded onto this scene breathing excitement and anticipation, tells Pistol that he, Falstaff, will 'deliver her' from the charge of murder. It is, as Dover Wilson quite reasonably describes it, a kind of madness[15] – hubris in search of nemesis.

The hypocrisy of King Hal – a necessary condition of power maintaining its moral dominance over poverty – is palpable even to Falstaff. But Falstaff, whose life of deceit has blinded him to the power of deceit, cannot recognize that Hal's hypocrisy is a permanent condition of his power. He knows that Hal's rejection is 'but a colour' (V,v,84); why should he not know it? He is a man of good instincts and intelligence. But he has devoted a great deal of his life to breaking down the separation of power and poverty, to discontaining the tavern and its madnesses, and calculates that this public declaration is the moment at which it all must happen. This is the risk of Falstaff's life as he claims the king as his own: 'my royal Hal!' (41), 'my sweet boy!' (42), 'My King! My Jove! I speak to thee, my heart!' (46). In this public place, in the presence of the nation itself, its power and might on the one hand contrasting with the ill-dressed ragtag of the tavern, Falstaff calls on the King to make his choice, to declare before the nation what its fate shall be.

That the rejection speech is a piece of blatant hypocrisy is certainly evident to Falstaff. His first words after Hal's speech indicate defeat: 'Master Shallow, I owe you a thousand pound' (73). The quick cover-up of, 'I shall be sent for in private' (77), does little to take away the effect of the first recognition of rejection which has been validated theatrically and politically by previous events to which the audience or reader have been privy. It is in that reference to his debt to Shallow that Falstaff makes acknowledgement of the ultimate triumph of the patriarchal polity and of his exclusion from it. What he owes Shallow must come, after all, not from the public coffers but from his own pocket. Falstaff has been separated from those institutions which maintain power. He is relegated to his place ten miles from the person of the king, and poverty and violence, having been authoritatively *named*, are restored to their safer places where they can be seen from a distance.

The public repudiation of Falstaff and those others whom Hal pleases to call his 'misleaders' is eloquent political discourse. To describe it as hypocrisy – which it surely is – is to neglect its brilliant efficacy as an example of the discourse of political order. It is part of a performance designed for a public panting for order. It is part of Hal's genius to have made them pant. He has generated among his subjects a fear of revolution, a fear of the conflation or the inversion of prose and verse and the worlds they separately stand for. The rejection speech and its charged emblematic background put paid to that fear. Power is retained by the king. The rule of hypocrisy which has become synonymous with the rule of order is re-entrenched. Hal's speech is a masterly example of the act of containment and separation. 'I have long dreamt of such a kind of man' (49) is an act of separation of illusion and reality. It reconstructs the 'real' as it separates the king's selves into a real and an illusory. As he has become king, the speech proclaims, Hal has been restored to the world of reality where poverty and patriarchy are and ought to be separate. 'I do despise my dream' (51) he states, reinforcing the notion of his former self as an unreal ephemeral self. *This* is now, this is the real me. And, of course, he goes further, makes the point explicit. 'Presume not that I am the thing I was' (56) is a declaration for one audience only – that audience onstage who have not been given repeated assurances of the underlying duplicity of Prince Hal. And it is that audience which requires the assurance that power has not changed purpose, that its interest is the same as those interests which have helped maintain it to this point. The moral issues of deception, friendship, loyalty are made subservient to the larger issue addressed in the drama, the issue of power's ability to identify and contain subversion and violence and to perpetuate itself and fortify its own institutions in the process. In its identification of the threat of violent subversion, authority in this play succeeds – as the ending eloquently shows – in displacing its own violent impulses and failures upon those least able to reply.

5

Monopolizing Violence: *Henry V*

In *Henry V*, finally, violence has become the handmaiden of
absolutist monarchy; it is employed by the monarch in the service
of order and success. The drama is thus a culmination of the fractious
disordered violence in the previous plays of the tetralogy where it
is a generalized implement in the quest for power. It is a truism
of that world of civil disharmony that control of the means of
violence is synonymous with the control of the monarchy. As the
monarchs and would-be monarchs of the previous three dramas
desire it, Henry V finally achieves total control of the physical and
metaphysical means of suppression. As the previous histories did
not, this play suppresses through ritual, comedy, satire, and silence
the disturbance and evil of violence. Thus the violence threatened
by the French armies and English villains like Pistol is never truly
threatening; it is marginalized as essentially harmless comic violence
or cowardly violence directed at children – indeed, the murder of
the boys is additional evidence of French pusillanimity. Positive,
socially valuable violence is entirely in the hands of King Henry.
It is effectively unchallenged.

By his uncanny political instincts and his use of the instruments
of power, Henry develops a tight grip on the political structure. He
knows and sees everything, not with the use of magic – though he
allows it to be thought that he has virtual shamanistic power – but
as a result of his control of the physical might of his nation. Part
of that control is maintained by his use of the individual subject's
multifaceted fear of the multiple 'other', so that the English are led
to assume that it is natural to hate and despise the French. He uses
fear as an agency of even benign control; the lengthy panegyrics of
the bishop and archbishop in the first scene are shown to derive in
part from the fear that Henry will appropriate property and rights

from the church. The ambiguity of the play will forever displace the attempts to demonize or deify this monarch. Yet his political success cannot be questioned and his methodical use of warfare as a means of cementing that success are the solid facts from which the drama springs. Warfare is both a global diversion, to busy giddy minds with foreign quarrels, *and* it is a means of proving in the hardest proving ground of all that this king has earned and deserves his title. Warfare is thus a kind of continuation of the ritual of blood he embraced as the Prince of Wales who once took a sacred vow to kill Hotspur, his father's greatest enemy. The English blood shed in these battles against France is dear to this king, but it is the necessary cost of this singularly difficult monarchy.

Henry is an example of what the anthropologists call the 'Big Man', a ruler who operates within a system that is largely designed to sustain a system of individual leadership and to privilege and encourage the value of individualism as a real political means of uniting the commonwealth. The 'Big Man' structure entails the dominance of 'a leader who will gather his own network of allegiances powerfully around himself and create a centre of force for the rest of society'.[1] Upon that centre rests the possibility of reassurance and peace. The variety of homages paid to Henry's capacities for leadership are evidences of the readiness of the political and cultural structures to support this system. As Gundersheimer and others have shown, the 'Big Man' must maintain his position of dominance by the use of power coupled with the use of patronage and by careful balancing of the two against each other. To be sure, Henry V is in control of the nation, but the maintenance of this control is possible because he manages skillfully to keep within his grasp the loyalty of his most powerful subjects by patronage. And, indeed, the most powerful body of his subjects – the ordinary soldiers – are kept in check by his masterly use of the power that gift-giving provides him with.

Another more abstract and metaphysical source of his control is revealed in the Scroop, Cambridge, and Grey incident where Henry instructs his subject audiences about the power of secret knowledge. He and the potent force of acquiescence within the drama imply that the knowledge has an almost magical source, but, in reality, it is obtained by the practice of spying, or as the wry and astute Bedford says, 'by interception which they dream not of' (II,ii,7). As today, when one person's terrorist is another's freedom fighter, so with Henry, the use of spies strikes a complicated chord. The practice itself may strike us as a necessary evil but, even in that fact, makes complex the whole construction of this king and his power. That is to say, Henry's very success, his total possession of that thing that all around him seem to want – absolute control and power – makes him axiomatically suspect. The performance-trial demonstrates clearly that his enemies are helpless before him, for he knows what they are thinking. Henry places into the conspirators' hands evidence of their treachery and warns meaningfully, 'know, I know your worthiness' (II,ii,69). The repetition of 'know' is charged with ominous implication.

This carefully stage-managed scene is a condensed example of the basic unit of action of the drama as a whole and of a number of similarly structured episodes within it. Here, as elsewhere, violent reprisal is justified in advance and is predetermined as morally correct because it is carried out by the dominant authority. This is an intelligent if machiavellian use of power, but it works when the determining force – the monarch – is recognized by the majority of his powerful subjects to be that very force. But here, as in other such incidents in the play, the act of justification is contingent and dependent on a prior set of principles, actions, and information which are not seen and which depend upon the authority of the monarch's word and the concomitant credulity of his audiences. The violent act of execution is publicly proven to be just and merciful by the accompanying ritual of confession which has the added value of promising salvation for the criminals. The confessions are powerful endorsements of the monarch's power. Like the Gardener scene of *Richard II*, this scene hides its contradictions under formalism and ritual. Careful dramatic orchestration and stylized coincidence give the episode the hard glossy veneer of absolute moral and political rectitude. The traitors go beyond acknowledging their baseness and treachery, they welcome their own violent deaths and celebrate the justice of their executioner. Scroop acknowledges the hand of divine justice in Henry's triumph:

> Our purposes God hath justly discovered
> And I repent my fault more than my death;
> Which I beseech your highness to forgive,
> Although my body pay the price for it.

> (II,iii,154–7)

The common belief in God – curiously and anxiously enforced by law – is a potent and useful tool of social cohesion for both authority and subject. The God of patriarchy who both punishes and forgives provides a means for traitors to return to society. And as they do so, as they reclaim God and their own salvation, they become entitled to recuperate the vocabulary that will officially reconnect them to the social formation which their crime has put beyond their reach. This belief in God by subjects and citizens endues the living monarch (or the dominant culture) with a power by which his own is given validity – it fortifies his actions with a sanction that even his enemies acknowledge – and it gives his enemies and victims a means to immortality. Scroop's words indicate his recognition of the connectedness of the king to God. He seeks forgiveness from the king as he welcomes physical death, hoping by his repentance to achieve at least spiritual healing which only the king's forgiveness can provide. The victim himself sanctions the violence that will kill him, and thus rounds off the performance/demonstration of the humanity and moral authority of the monarch. The victims in this scene are willing sacrificial victims of society.

Henry's performance here, with its highly stylized linguistic and histrionic mode, supplies the incident with the ingredients of a sanctioned ritual of social cleansing. The three noblemen who are more valuable to the text's pro-Henry ideology as victims because they are noblemen, offer themselves up upon the altar of patriarchal monarchy. Their conspiracy against the king is transformed into a more potent conspiracy *with* the king in demonstrating his publicly perceived flawlessness. The incidents of the play and the public professions and perceptions of Henry are all dramatic indications of his heroic invulnerability. The stylization of this scene is the work not of Henry, of course, but of his maker. Thus it is that Henry himself, however conscious, deliberate, or scheming he may strike us, is nevertheless himself subject to a larger force than himself, the rhyming poet who lends to the scene the substantial aura of a ritual. Thus, though the scene is a naked exercise of power, its and the whole play's notorious undecidability derive from the clash of action with style. In losing spontaneity, and acquiring the rhythmical pattern of a practiced ceremony, the text is enclosed in a ritualism whose purpose can be understood as a quasi-sacred vindication of the monarch and a temporary suspension of the opposing forces of subversion; it is another example of the travel between subversion and validation that so complicates the play, for seldom (not never) do the two impulses work simultaneously here as they do in the previous plays of the tetralogy. Instead the tendency is towards serial representation of the political alternatives embedded in the action – the unambiguous Chorus being the most palpable example.

In this incident conventional wisdom, reason, and morality harmonise to provide a motive for a sacrificial violence in behalf of social order. This confluence is a paradigm for the significant actions of the drama. A major point of significance of the present example is the passionate willingness of the victim-traitors to die acknowledging the justice of the hand that smites them down. Elsewhere in the play, however, matters are less cohesive or morally neat. And it is these cases that make the acts of legitimate violence and absolute control more ambiguous. Though the reader is exhorted by the chorus and such tidy and one-dimensional actions as the arrest of the traitors to recognize no such ambiguity, some actions have the effect of producing a moral uncertainty that precisely challenges the 'Official Version'[2] of events. Tyranny is seen as just rule when the means of social and political oppression are tied to the social value of order: tyranny is seen as tyranny when the means of social and political oppression are seen as social and political oppression. Perception, that is, is ideological and partial and contingent on the way in which the perceiver apprehends his/her relation to the dominant power.

Henry V, as Ely and Canterbury delightedly remind themselves, is a master of persuasion:

> Hear him but reason in divinity . . .
> Hear him debate of commonwealth affairs . . .
> List his discourse of war . . .
> Turn him to any course of policy . . .
> . . . when he speaks,
> The air, a charter'd libertine, is still,
> And the mute wonder lurketh in men's ears,
> To steal his sweet and honey'd sentences.
>
> (I,i,38–50)

The complexity of this passage as rhetoric in its own right is part of the difficulty of the play. The fact that the churchmen stand to gain by the war makes them suspect – arouses disbelief; how, on the other hand, do we account for the passion in their praises, their pleasure in Henry's rhetoric as rhetoric? Though it may be a passion that owes something to self-interest, it is represented as authentically felt, and thus warns us against a rather too simple vilification of the Church and the King. Ambiguity remains an uncomfortable fact inextricably embedded in the linguistic structure of the drama. The Churchmen are integrally connected by policy and necessity to the order the king embodies. As divinity, government, warfare, and policy can be made to sound sweetly reasonable, so violence itself can be made a part of the same structure of reason so long as its rationalization and justification fall within the limitations of the dominant rhetoric. For it is the dominant culture which tends to monopolize modes of rationality and thus to define and determine reason, to justify national policy and action. There is, furthermore, a single dangerous fact that lies at the heart of the play, a fact which the text seems to acknowledge but which only the interestingly marginal Williams evidently recognizes. That fact is the simple possibility of tyranny by a monarch who possesses so much power; that possibility is expressed through the various fears of some subjects: the fears of the churchmen, the fears of the traitors, the fears of ordinary soldiers all have in common a fear of the power of this king.

Most collectivities acknowledge the existence of and distinction between cohesive and ruptural (to use the Althusserian term) violence. Cohesive violence, as we have seen, tends to be that which serves the dominant culture, while ruptural violence subverts it. The criminalization of violent acts is, in this light, a political decision by the dominant authority. Crime itself, exemplified specifically *as* crime in this play is individualized in order that its political force be minimized; it is constructed by the dominant authority as danger-ous to all elements of the social formation regardless of their relation to the ruling fraction. But, of course, it is that very ruling fraction which has most to gain from the general apprehension of crime as a threat to social stability: that is, unlawful violence threatens us all while lawful violence protects us all is a nearly universal social code (Bardolph steals a pyx, Henry executes him). What 'society' is said to regard as the distinction between the two kinds of violence is what the dominant element of society determines to be the distinc-tion. That distinction within the play is entirely determined by King Henry in his deeds and words. As monarch he possesses the right to make the socially crucial distinction. Thus, when he adopts the language of violent threat outside Harfleur, for example, the threats themselves become sanitized because it is he who is making them. It is possible to justify Henry's use of these threats only because they are never realized. Yet the deferred reality behind them is precisely what scares the citizens. Thus, again, Henry stands squarely in the centre of ambiguity, having done a good thing by a bad means. The text will not permit a solution to this typical dilemma.

Many people have recognized in the doubts of Michael Williams one of the most probing points of subversion in the play. A man of no authority confronts a disguised king; speaking in the voice of the ordinary soldier he sabotages the rationalizations of Ely, Canterbury, and Henry. *Their* war is predicated upon a just cause casuistically developed. Williams doesn't care. To Henry's anxious irony, 'I could not die any where so contented as in the king's company, his cause being just and his quarrel honorable,' Williams offers the rejoinder, 'That's more than we know' (II, i, 128–30). The action is the king's attempt to bridge the distance between himself and his men. Coming in disguise amongst them, he raises on the one hand the possibility of his being like them, a man with fears and doubts. On the other hand, the disguise itself is his protection because it is temporary, because he can remove it at will and smash their subversion whenever he pleases. He is reminiscent in this power of the Duke of *Measure for Measure* whose use of disguise has occasioned so much moral doubt. That is, Henry's tyranny (real or potential) is nowhere so evident as when he hides it in a cloak, for in doing so he retains the power to entrap and surprise subversion by deception, being himself potent and subversive. The outcome of this episode – including Henry's evasion of Williams's hostile questioning – vividly and dramatically restores the distance between the man of authority and the man with none just as it ostensibly bridges it. Henry forgives Williams because he is able to deflect his potential subversion and render it ineffectual; he gives money to him in an exchange for his soldierly loyalty. With money it is possible to grease the machinery of violent conquest. The gesture of giving money to a subordinate is determined in a consistent, unchanging social complex of implication from which there can be no release within patriarchal political structures. The thousands of examples in literature of a rich man giving money to a poor or poorer man always reconfirm the evidence of their relative relations to institutional power and restate semiotically their interest in that power's longevity.

Anne Barton has pointed out that this gift of Henry's, 'unlike its archtypes in the ballads and in Elizabethan comical histories, seems strangely irrelevant. Consciously anachronistic, it provides not the ghost of an answer to the questions raised during this particular encounter between common man and king disguised'.[3] Charity – of which this gesture is a clear form – is a deeply embedded practice within the culture that produced and inherited this play. Royal munificence, as shown by Coppelia Kahn, is designed to serve both the emotional needs of the gift-giver and, in this play especially, his political designs.[4]

Henry is like the gift-givers and patrons discussed by Kahn in being the chief source of unreciprocated liberality. By this means he establishes his political and paternal superiority which is only further validated when Williams accepts the glove full of crowns from the king. The absence of spoken gratitude or thanks signify secret resentment and is emphasised when he proudly declines to participate in Fluellen's imitation of the king's patronage. In Williams's refusal of Fluellen's shilling resides a whole social history of rank- and class-based resentment which illuminates one of the more unpalatable givens of the play: that is, surely, a potential contradiction between the interests of the ruler and his subjects. Williams's surly rebuff to Fluellen is a symbolic gesture of repudiation of the same politics that force him to accept the king's glove of crowns. The offering by Henry is a gestural recuperation of the discrepancy between rich and poor, between powerful people and powerless people which his night adventure had temporarily broken down. But more, it fills a need that the patriarchal monarchical ideologies determine. It satisfies desire and want just as it restates their constant presence as a factor in the lives of such as Williams whose place in society predetermines financial need as a condition of his existence.

Charity is only another form of patronage. There is no real distinction between the act of giving charity and that of supplying patronage. In each case the giver receives – indeed the giver cannot help receiving, even when he does his good by stealth. For charity is one of the most visible and obvious means of maintaining the political system which supports the ideology that valorizes it. That is, charity is obviously designed to maintain the structure that makes the practice necessary, for the act of charity purchases the obedience, loyalty, and deference of the persons who are *made* to depend on it. This is not to argue that no-one ever gives without the expectation of a return, but rather that the social and cultural structures of society make it impossible not to receive a return by the act of giving. This fact might explain the attractions of this aspect of our culture which represents charity as an absolute value. Patronage – especially that practiced by such people as James I and such characters as Timon of Athens – is a form of charity to the rich. It too secures loyalty, obedience, and love which can, in turn, be transformed, as Machiavelli shows, into effective instruments of violent suppression.

The commencement of *Henry V* with an elaborate defense of the use of violence by two clerics produces a characteristic language of oppression for this play. It is a language that glorifies violence by projecting it as a means of consecrating the monarchy. The use of the church here – whatever we wish to think of the individual churchmen – has a potent gestural and rhetorical force:

> Awake remembrance of these valiant dead,
> And with your puissant arm renew their feats!
> You are their heir; you sit upon their throne;
> The blood and courage that renowned them
> Runs in your veins.

> (I,ii,115–19)

There is purpose too in the regular appearances of the Chorus, whose immense control of the moral direction of the events is used to consolidate the heroic by representing violence as exciting and necessary – as anything, in short, but nasty and brutish. But Williams's skepticism has the effect of undermining precisely this tie between God, the church, and the king. Scroop's acknowledgement that Henry's is a godlike voice and authority, propounded and reinforced by Ely and Canterbury, is thrown into doubt by Williams's doubt. The honest soldier doing his job of killing other men would like to believe that it is a good job. He has no choice in the matter: 'if these men do die well, it will be a black matter for the king that led them to it, who to disobey were against all proportion of subjection' (IV,i,146–9). Henry's reply will not satisfy everyone: 'Every subject's duty is the king's; but every subject's soul is his own' (182–4). Norman Rabkin points out that the king's answer evades the issue: 'the suffering he is capable of inflicting, the necessity of being sure that the burden is imposed for a worthy cause.'[5]

The play keeps returning to this theme of the great gap that lies between the king and his subjects, from the stalwart Fluellen to the renegade Bardolph. The convenient image of the great chain of being aptly describes the means of monarchical patriarchal authority that is Henry's base of power. For the dominant authority to stress that its occupation is part of the larger scheme of things, that it has the sanction of the more mysterious authority of God, is to use effectively the considerable instruments of power which it commands. The sense that the head that wears the crown carries the greater burden of political responsibility, that by extension it is a wiser head, that it is a closer head to God's, suffuses the whole of Henry's discourse of justification. It is equally true, however, that this king takes upon himself the greater burdens, and places before himself the greater obstacles. His father's famous words, 'Uneasy lies the head that wears the crown', are validated by this king, searching for peace and justification. He finds these through bloody victory. He proves himself in the smithy of battle, a ritualized and time-honored means of solidifying patriarchal authority.

The great 'Once more unto the breach' speech is one of the superlative instances of the capacity of power to absorb and unite the social collectivity into itself. Though the speech is a flagrant glorification of violence and carnage, its disguise is the tantalizing offer to every ordinary soldier of his own private share in the king's glory. Through warfare alone does the ordinary Englishman of this world have the possibility of greatness in a life otherwise hungry and tough; for though the speech is addressed to the king's 'dear friends', in its details it addresses one soldier or, rather, each soldier individually. It appeals to the dominant ethic of individual achievement as it separates the single soldier from the mass. Reading the speech it is easy to forget that soldiers are united far more by a common fear of a hostile army than by the grandiloquent words of their leader. This speech cannot be read by many people separately from the memory of Lawrence Olivier's declamation of it in the film. It is about the glory to be purchased from combat, about the heroism available to all who hear it and in which all who hear it have been schooled, about the evanescent possibility of greatness within the grasp of every individual present; but above all it is about the transformation of the individual capacity for violence into a collective force of virile and heroic destruction. It is, further, about the common bond of war formed by men in danger and it supplies, thereby, one of the oldest justifications of the patriarchy.

This speech, a central moment in the play, is as rich in what it

implies as in what it says. The best women of this war are the
mothers of these English men who, it is suggested, bred these
men so that they could be present at this moment in this place.
Henry appeals to 'his men' in this speech, reconstituting them in
senses which flatter his hearers but have nothing to do with their
lives outside the battlefield: they are his 'dear friends', they are
absorbed into the king's personal orbit, hearing the war with 'our
ears'; they are the 'noblest English'. Indeed, the king appeals to their
masculinity with a specifically phallologic appeal to his soldiers
which urges them to let their eyes 'pry through the portage of the
head / Like the brass cannon' (III,i,10–11). The play which appears
to flourish such rhetoric flamboyantly and exultantly, also produces
an odd contradiction to that of Henry's English army so apparently
united in purpose and determination. The very next scene, a scene
of the battle itself with alarums and '*Soldiers with scaling ladders*'
[stage directions], far from demonstrating the mighty resolves of
the speech, instead shows confusion of purpose, disarray, mixture
of motive, inversion of rank, uncertainty of direction. This scene
shows the human side of the fighting machine so carefully crafted
by the king's imagery. It is in such dramatic demonstrations as this,
the scene of the battle itself, that the king's task is the hardest. Henry
has time and again to pick up the dropped threads of patriarchal
monarchy and put them into the 'right' order.

The speech, which flaunts Henry's English Christian militarism,
resonates in that following scene of its realization. As Henry lov-
ingly constructed the image of his men fighting a glorious battle for
the sake of God, St. George, England, her king, and their own mothers, so the actuality of that performance is represented as a violent
parody of the heroic representations in the king's speech. The effect
of this parody is to expose and subvert the optimism of the heroic
image that the play has so carefully developed. Bardolph, Nym,
Pistol and the Boy respond to the stirring speech by expressing
the 'cowardly' desire to be back in England – as Bates later wishes
himself up to the neck in the Thames. The prosaic realism of the
scene radically challenges the static and iconic effect of Henry's
exhortation, where the strategies of presentation conspire to make
the reader and audience forget the complex history of Henry/Hal's
accession and all its entangled personal and political conflicts. Thus
the scene that follows Henry's exhortation refutes the very image it
produces. James R. Siemon describes the process as a clash of iconic
and iconoclastic impulses: 'the dramatic icon of militant English

Christianity is seriously challenged by the work of art in which it is set.'[6]

The rousing cry, 'God for Harry, England, and Saint George!' (III,i,34) is followed immediately by alarums and chambers going off and *Bardolph* faking heroic rage ('he is white-liver'd and red-faced' III,ii,32) with his copycat travesty of Henry's call to arms – 'On, on, on, on! to the breach, to the breach!' (III,ii,1). The dramatic effect is a kind of satire on the illusion of total control of his men which Henry's speech created. Nym, Bardolph, Pistol, and the Boy are as poor representatives of the yeoman of England the play could have provided. Bardolph's words are the last he is to speak before he is executed.

The speech to the citizens of Harfleur is a curious, no doubt tactical, inversion of the speech before the battle. The earlier speech, as I have said, attempts to create an illusion of an army of English soldiers united in purpose with their king. Henry's images suggest a taut, disciplined fighting force awaiting their leader's command. To the citizens Henry describes these same valiant soldiers as a gang of ruffians and rapists incapable of being controlled. Each speech is an acknowledgement of the omnipotence of violence in the play. Violence itself, rather than the king's own morality, determines the means of its use. If violence is the key to success, then it is to violence that the king tacitly pays homage in each address. The inherent moral excellence of his troops developed in the first speech gives way to an image of these same troops as possessing a propensity for vicious excesses in the second. Success alone matters, and success can be accomplished only through the exercise of a violence whose legitimacy is ensured by the king who harnesses it. Henry acknowledges and uses the ideas of good and bad violence in the two speeches; he exploits the fact that they precisely contradict each other. To him, in pursuit of victory, there is but one justification and one moral principle; that is the principle of success as sufficient reason in and of itself. To the citizens of Harfleur violence is annihilation and death. The soldier who fights for this king is an extravagant and demonic force of destructive energy, 'With conscience wide as hell, mowing like grass / Your fresh fair virgins and your flowering infants' (III,iii,12–13). Henry's 'Once more unto the breach' exhortation is a brilliant representation of violent action as glorious action. The speech does not overtly supply a moral validation of the act of war, but rather seeks that justification only in its last line. The acts of killing which the king calls for are contingent for their rightness on the circumstance of the socially determined structure of the leadership of this king and the subservience of his soldiers. His exhortation, that is, derives its authority from the basic conditions of kingship which in this play, Anne Barton reminds us, derive from 'a complicated, inherently tragic Tudor doctrine of the king's two bodies'.[7] The violence with which he threatens the citizens of Harfleur, on the other hand, he clearly distinguishes from the violence of his rallying cry to his men.

The two speeches employ the idea of the woman in contrasting ideological forms which betray a troubling contradiction within the patriarchal structure of the play, and which the representations of Katherine ultimately and definitively validate. Within the framework of violent conquest to which all parts of the play – political and personal – are integrally connected, the mostly unseen English and French women are constituted again and again as essentially passive agents of male aggression. On the one hand they are the mothers who gave birth to the English soldiers who then become the repositories of national honour. On the other they are the French virgins who provide the evidence of English dishonour and French defeat by being raped by English soldiers. Henry's pornographic representations of 'pure maidens [falling] into the hand / Of hot and forcing violation' (20–1) and of 'shrill-shrieking daughters' (35) being violated by enraged (!) soldiers bring into conjunction the complementary ideas of sexuality and violence – 'licentious wickedness' (22). His method of persuasion in the speech to the citizens of Harfleur is strongly reminiscent of Iago's exhortation to Brabantio to look to his daughter because she and the Moor are making the two-backed beast; Othello is 'tupping' Desdemona, a description which suggests sex as a grotesque act of deformation repeatedly described in terms of violent male aggression. Henry's appalling threat includes that cliché of the iconography of conquest, the innocent virgin being raped by an alien conqueror. Such menaces are designed to warn the enemy that defeat is completed by humiliation and degradation. This form of violence in the play – the violence of conquest and rape – brings closer the relationship of sexuality and power that is hinted at or explicit in the language of the text.

The point is made again and again in the farce scenes of the play where violent language is fortified by sexual imagery. Where lovemaking is represented as a form of aggression not easily distinguishable from rape. In these plays about political power, sexuality is repeatedly represented as another manifestation of the relation of authority to its subjects. Sex is something men do to women, and the accompanying rituals – like wooing – are represented, particularly in this play's wooing scene, as trite political conventions. Through wooing, women are given the illusion of their own power to participate in the ritual. But the fact is otherwise, as is clearly shown when hearty Harry throws himself at Kate's feet. No scene better demonstrates the powerlessness of the female than this one and demonstrates, simultaneously, the silent conspiracy to pretend that she is not powerless. But, as is the case with the poor and the merely ordinary men of the play, the woman's function is to demonstrate the unicentricity of the king's power. Henry's ostensible embarrassment, awkwardness, and stagey bluffness are part of the convention by which the illusion of female power is sustained. It is all of piece with the performance of wooing which is part of the larger structure of representation of the recuperated control of authority into the immediate sphere of the monarch.

Jonathan Dollimore and Alan Sinfield make the point that *Henry V*'s obsessive preoccupation is insurrection: 'The King is faced with actual or threatened insurrection from almost every quarter: the Church, "treacherous" fractions within the ruling class, slanderous subjects, and soldiers who undermine the war effort.'[8] Because women are not a class, but rather one of the accoutrements of class, they are not part of the general pattern of potential subversion. The wooing scene shows Henry at his most confident, although throughout he persistently asserts his diffidence. Katherine's role, however, is predetermined, the result a foregone conclusion adumbrated by the scenes in which she learns English to the accompaniment of fairly amusing, prurient giggling as she wonders about this interesting English king. In short, the text makes her unambiguously frivolous – she doesn't have a chance to be taken seriously, and her plight as a woman about to be bartered in marriage and used for mating is trivialized. Thus, the declarations of his plain-spokenness and unsophistication are – like all his voices in the play – strategy against subversion. The contradictions between the assertions of this scene are palpably at odds with the canny political manoeuverings of such earlier episodes as, for example, the betrayal scene. Dover Wilson's apologia for Henry rests on the moral asseveration that the king, wooing, was fulfilling ultimately all of the promise of Hal. His courtship reveals him as the man he insists he is – the blunt 'soldier genuinely in love, but to whom integrity of mind and plain dealing are the very pith of life .... May we not even guess it to be the kind of wooing Shakespeare himself admired?'[9] But the courtship can equally be seen as an inevitable part of the whole project of the containment of insurrection. Through his marriage to Katherine, the greatest potential source of violent overthrow comes under Henry's own sway. The French King offers his daughter to Henry as a token of the agreement between the two monarchs, as evidence of Henry's ultimate control of the might of both Christian countries:

> Take her, fair son; and from her blood raise up
> Issue to me; that the contending kingdoms
> Of France and England, whose very shores look pale
> With envy of each other's happiness,
> May cease their hatred, and this dear conjunction
> Plant neighbourhood and Christian-like accord
> In their sweet bosoms, that never war advance
> His bleeding sword 'twixt England and fair France.
>
> (V,ii,366–74)

The match of Henry and Katherine is dramatically designed to *look like* a 'dear conjunction' in order to sustain the image of Henry's overwhelming charisma. This scene shows a nation of fighting French transformed into the tame dinner guests of their new monarch, almost as though they had been eagerly waiting to be defeated so that they could subject themselves to him.

Of all the instruments of national cohesion which Henry V employs, none is so powerful and constant as the instrument of Christianity. From the first scene, with the two powerful churchmen offering a plethora of ostensibly valid Christian reasons for supporting the king in his pursuit of national unification by war, Christianity as a tool of authority looms largest. Its signifiers are everywhere – they are embedded in the language through direct reference, in the gestures, and in the iconic representations of the play. A legion of readers has noted the fraudulence of the Archbishop and the Bishop's reasoning. Ralph Berry has described the dialogue of churchmen as a 'parcel of non-sequiturs' and noted that it is 'rhetoric designed to embellish a predetermined policy, and identifiable as fustian'.[10] The power of their argument lies in their apparent proprietorship of the ideology that lends authority to what they say. Thus, the cooperation of the church matters to Henry as he pursues his intention of expanding the empire he rules. His cleverness is his demonstration to the Church that it needs him to sustain its own sway.

The language of religion is almost all England's and Henry's. Of the fifty-nine uses of 'God' in the play, only three are by Frenchmen. Of the seven uses of 'Christ', 'Christian', and 'Christian-like', none are by Frenchmen. God is made to seem, by virtue of this monopolised reiteration, to belong to the English; the responsibility for the violence and aggression of the war is displaced onto the implicitly Godless French subjects of attack. He sanctions violence through his agencies of authority on earth. On the one – the primary – level of this play, Henry is the Christian king *par excellence*. In part this representation is achieved through the constant implication that the Christianity of the French is pallid. In Henry himself is concentrated the sacramental function. His appropriation of religious authority is manifested in the appropriation of the priestly role. In France we see him invoking God, blessing, confessing and absolving his men. His authority increases with his usurpation of the functions of the churchmen.

The Chorus, another powerful voice of authority, is, paradoxically, evidence of anxiety. His function is to diminish contradiction, to enable illusion and, supremely, to make palatable the violent means by which the hero wins his empire. He is a guide through the tangle of potential doubt which the actions of Henry produce. He goads, tempts, taunts, and entices the audience to see beyond what it can see, taking them behind the scenes to the vaster area, the bigger picture. In doing so he supplies information which cannot be verified except through himself, leaving the audience entirely dependent on his word for what passes before it. Thus, as the Chorus possesses the unassailable, unchallengeable, and unchallenged authority to make an audience see what is not there, so he appropriates the moral authority of mentor. Established, that is, as a kind of tour guide to the imagination, he becomes, by a logical extension of that function, an interpreter as well. His crying up of 'Harry' is well known. He is, as Berry puts it, 'the Official Version of the events culminating in Agincourt'.[11] The discrepancy between his version of events and the drama itself is the evidence of the play's continuous anxiety. A deep tension binds the two narratives – those of Chorus and play – as each refracts the other. One of the functions of the Chorus, for example, is to play down the caricature of the French that the dramatic narrative supplies. In the Chorus's version of the scene before the battle of Agincourt, the foregone conclusion of an English victory against its effete enemy is far less determined than the dramatic narrative alone proposes. It is true that the English are 'low-rated' (IV, *Chorus*, 19) and the French 'confident and over-lusty' (18), but the sense of a real battle and real risk suffuse the Chorus's description of a 'dreadful' preparation: while the representations of the dramatic narrative makes the French a pack of fools, the Chorus corrects that impression in order to lend value to the English victory.

The glory of the victory issues from the fact that the reins of violence are held by a king whose hold precisely indicates a complex of Christian rectitude, social order, and a vertical structure of power relationships. The other side of this coin – immorality, social deformation, and an inverted power structure where violence is under the control of the poor and the ordinary – is projected comically through the megalomaniacal Pistol as 'wrong' or insane. Conquest and control, domestic and external, are the products of an ideological system which valorizes hierarchical forms of government through a host of well established formulae supported and sustained for centuries. The society is shot through with varieties of violence whose practices have evolved through the social tremors of conflict, resistance, and domination. A pervasive argument of this play is that the instruments of violence have fallen, through struggle, into the 'right' hands. That 'rightness', it has been argued, owes more to the ideology of success than to that of absolute moral truth. The tetralogy of plays to which *Henry V* belongs attempts, on one level, to demonstrate the workings of an historical process which results inevitably, even naturally, in the monarchy of Henry V. What the plays have not suppressed is the persistent series of contradictions which subvert the very idea of that process.

6

The Rape of Lavinia

In three of Shakespeare's tragedies women protagonists are killed by men. In *Titus Andronicus* Lavinia is killed by her father; in *Othello* Desdemona is killed by her husband; in *King Lear* Cordelia is killed by a soldier. While the killing of Cordelia is represented as a cruelly unmotivated murder, Lavinia and Desdemona are killed precisely in order to sustain masculine ideals of honour which each woman is represented as having challenged or exposed. The death of Desdemona follows from her being perceived as willfully unfaithful to the masculine code of sexual fidelity.

Lavinia is a more complex case. Her innocence is known and affirmed by every character in the play, including her father who eventually kills her. Her conduct is under no suspicion, yet to her father and the emperor of Rome she is dishonoured. Once it is publicly known that Lavinia has been raped, she is understood to have been shamed. Titus asks Emperor Saturninus:

> Was it well done of rash Virginius
> To slay his daughter with his own right hand,
> Because she was enforc'd, stain'd, and deflower'd?
>   *Sat.*   It was, Andronicus.
>   *Tit.*   Your reason, mighty lord.
>   *Sat.*   Because the girl should not survive her shame,
> And by her presence still renew his sorrows.
>   *Tit.*   A reason mighty, strong, and effectual;
> A pattern, president, and lively warrant
> For me, most wretched, to perform the like.
> Die, die, Lavinia, and thy shame with thee;
> And with thy shame thy father's sorrow die!
>   [*He kills her.*] (V,iii, 36–47)

It is obviously true that Saturninus and Titus are far from exemplary guides to moral behaviour, and yet the execution of Lavinia, who passively and unresistingly collaborates in her own killing, is carried out with an almost iconic simplicity. It is an action that is represented – like so much else in this rather mad play – as another emblematic example of wild justice that the drama seethes with.

That is to say the murder of Lavinia is only part of a larger pattern through which the drama of Titus Andronicus is seen to acquire the force and finality of a reenacted play. And the play's repeated intertextual intertwinings and allusions lend the death of Lavinia the moral force of mythical and political precedent. In his study of the myth of Lucretia, Ian Donaldson makes the point that this myth, which is surely sustained by *Titus Andronicus*, is 'a mythology invented, sustained, and extended largely by men. It is significant', he adds, 'that the number of women who have chosen to treat this subject in literature and the visual arts is exceedingly small'.[1] He goes on to discuss the cultural equation of rape and adultery, an equation which is overtly supported by the ethos of *Titus*, though vehemently rejected by the maniacally rebellious Tamora. Donaldson argues that in the society in which Lucretia lived, 'Sexual intercourse between a wife and a man other than her husband was seen in this time as an act which mysteriously and irretrievably tainted the woman concerned. No distinction was made in this matter between adultery and rape, for the polluting effect of both acts was thought to be the same.'[2] Shakespeare's text appears to comply with this cultural determinant, though a ferocious resistance to such moral certainty and simplicity is mounted by Tamora.

Patriarchy renews itself – with a self-conscious nod at heroic tragic necessity – through the killing of an innocent woman. The play abandons questions of moral uncertainty in the first scene. There is no place here for moral shock or ethical questioning. From the beginning, with the first onstage killing, a kind of ethical anarchy becomes the hallmark of the plot. Such a condition is possible only in a world where contrasts are stark and immediate. Black and white stand out in vivid opposition. In such a world the clash of opposites is the source of a drama of conflict; the implications of good and evil or right and wrong are almost uninteresting, giving way as they do to the more exacting matter of the means through which the conflict is expressed.

For all the bloodletting in *Titus Andronicus*, for all the crazy mutilation, killing, and cannibalism, the truly haunting and frightening image of the play is that of the mute and handless Lavinia seeking the means to express herself. As a character with a voice, as she is initially, Lavinia is no more nor less interesting and potent than any other character in the drama. As the mangled remnant of the character she once was, flailing her stumps in the air, she assumes a new magnitude. She becomes the cynosure of all eyes, the subject of all speech, and the central object of attention whenever she is onstage. As those who love her attempt to articulate the wordless sounds she makes, so she becomes the source of their greatest challenge as they seek to become her voice, to shape her thoughts into language. But their efforts are fruitless, and it is not until Lavinia circumvents her silent fate and writes the names of her attackers in the sand that they become identified. Lawrence Danson has argued that *Titus Andronicus* is 'a play about silence, and about the inability to achieve adequate expression for overwhelming emotional needs'.[3] In this silence itself, Lavinia fulfills a male ideal of virtue. Peter Stallybrass notes that 'Silence, the closed mouth, is made a sign of chastity. And silence and chastity are, in turn, homologous to woman's enclosure within the house.'[4] And indeed the huge excesses that characterize the language and the actions are sure indices of a passionate need to speak, a need which the male characters act upon because they have male freedom, but which in women is repressed, as is brutally signified in Lavinia's specifically and wholly female plight.

It is Lavinia who provides the evidence of these inadequacies. She is raped by Chiron and Demetrius – with the connivance of their mother and Aaron – then her tongue is cut out and her hands cut off. She attempts in this state to give the names of her assailants but cannot, for a long while, find the means to do so. Eventually she holds a stick between her stumps and writes their names in the sand. It is only after her father has taken revenge on those who raped her that she is killed by him. This is an interesting point. The worst thing that happens to Lavinia, by far, is the rape. The mutilations are incidental to it, both in the minds of the perpetrators and in those of her own family. This is not to say that the mutilations are not taken seriously, but rather that they are adjunctive to the rape. They are equivalent to the violences done to the men, sadistic and pragmatic, but nonsexual. They are mere evidences of brutality while rape is evidence of a brutal violation that affects not just the victim, and not just her family and friends, but the society as a whole. It is the nature of the ensuing dishonour – the way that it is given form – that is so revealing. Merely to know of Lavinia's rape is to be compelled by that knowledge into moral decision. And the unanimous and completely unchallenged decision in this case is that Lavinia has

been made into an object of proven dishonour. By being raped she
has acquired a moral taint. It is probably not remarkable, but it is
shocking, that no single character in the play – none of her brothers,
her uncle, her father – propose that she remains innocent despite her
rape, an omission that implicates them in a collaboration with the
dominant ethic which declares rape to be soilure and inseparable
in effect from infidelity. No fact more powerfully than this insists
on Lavinia's status as an object. For a man to bring down such an
evaluation upon himself by his family and his society he needs to
commit a heinous crime, like treason. A woman has only to be
known to have been raped and her integrity is destroyed.

Titus Andronicus continues a tradition – one which was to last
until at least the nineteenth century – in which the victim of rape
was normally depicted as beyond social recovery and fit only for
seclusion or death.[5] Madelon Gohlke argues that the rape metaphor
supplies the idea that violence against women as 'an aspect of the
structure of male dominance in Shakespeare's plays may be seen to
obscure deeper patterns of conflict in which women as lovers, and
perhaps more importantly as mothers, are perceived as radically
untrustworthy. In this structure of relation, it is women who are
regarded as powerful and men who strive to avoid an awareness
of their vulnerability in relation to women, a vulnerability in which
they regard themselves as "feminine."'[6] There is, surely, something
crucial about the remarkable persistence of this ideological structure within a world where, after all, women were raped and still
permitted back into the social network. Rape, it seems, is the worst
fate available for a woman. And rape in bourgeois literature carries
with it the penalty of death for the victim. The victim of rape is
always a chaste woman – a virgin or a faithful, loving wife; while the
plays of the sixteenth, seventeenth, and eighteenth centuries abound
with promiscuous women, it is never a promiscuous woman who is
raped. Since part of the inherent purpose of rape onstage is to defile
as well as injure the victim, it is not possible to defile a woman
who already has sexual experience outside marriage. This practice
of making women the determinants of social and patriarchal purity,
endues them with a huge social responsibility as it reflects the
fragility of the structure that so depends upon them.

Paradoxically, the social and legal prohibition upon rape is the
very thing that makes it such a powerful incentive to the rapist. To
rape a woman, an act within the power of most men, is to reinforce
the man's sense of his own power. For not only does rape declare

the physical power of the man over the woman, but also, in circumstances such as those of the plays, it restates his ability to drive her from society. That is, his social and political power over women is affirmed by the way she is shunned. The essential masculineness of the idea of rape as soilure is confirmed by the unanimous agreement of all those concerned that rape is synonymous with taint. On this point the rapist and the victim's own family, and apparently even the victim herself, are in agreement. It is as though inerasable dirt has attached itself to the victim, notwithstanding the universal and unambiguous moral condemnation of rape. In *Titus Andronicus* and the three other English rape dramas written between 1594 and 1612, the heroines all die, despite their universally acknowledged innocence.[7]

As it is presented in *Titus Andronicus*, rape is shown to have to do with power relations between men and women and, perhaps less predictably, men and men. Lavinia's very body is the site of a political conflict among men seeking power. Upon that body is inscribed in horrible detail the evidence of the success of one side in this conflict. The inscription – cropping the hands and tongue from the body – creates an icon of silence; it leaves no trace of rape upon the body but prevents the tongue and hands from telling the rape. The rape of a married woman like Lavinia is an act of secrecy which leaves no visible evidence of its having happened. There is no virginal blood to mark the legs of the victim, no sexual sign of the rape. Yet Marcus, Lavinia's uncle, knows that she has been raped because she averts her face from his gaze in shame, and blushes before the gaze of men which seems able to penetrate her mind:

> Why dost not speak to me?
> Alas a crimson river of warm blood,
> Like to a bubbling fountain stirr'd with wind,
> Doth rise and fall between thy rosed lips,
> Coming and going with thy honey breath.
> But sure, some Tereus hath deflower'd thee,
> And, lest thou should'st detect him, cut thy tongue.
> Ah, now thou turn'st away thy face for shame,
> And notwithstanding all this loss of blood,
> As from a conduit with three issuing spouts,
> Yet do thy cheeks look red as Titan's face
> Blushing to be encount'red with a cloud.
>
> (II,iv,21–32)

The blushes of Lavinia are silent signifiers of guilt. Blushing is a weakness of whiteness, and yet, in this powerful, masculine Roman world spoiled by 'others' – women and blacks – whiteness is also a virtuous hue because it can expose guilt and shame. Aaron reminds Chiron:

> Why, there's the privilege your beauty bears.
> Fie, treacherous hue, that will betray with blushing
> The close enacts and counsels of thy heart!
>
> (IV,ii,116–18)

Lavinia's dreadfully deformed body becomes a text exploding with signs. The physical destruction of Lavinia is a message fraught with significance. That men have maimed her is immediately and automatically assumed; that she has been sexually assaulted is verified by the look of shame that her blushing signifies. The reddened cheeks speak of her guilt; her body is giving spontaneous expression to a kind of complicity with her rapists. So, it is not only the men who recognize the culpability of the victim, but also the victim herself who blushes at her part in the degradation as if she were, in very truth, like the revealed traitor whose act has compromised his family and society. This is a powerful message, and represents to us, in large measure, the extent to which the woman's subjection has been regarded as a given and a moral right in Western culture. Shakespeare himself and his plays have often been the site of conflicts about social value and cultural determinations. Lavinia's body, says Tennenhouse, 'provides the setting for political rivalry among the various families with competing claims to power over Rome. For one of them to possess her is for that family to display its power over the rest.'[8]

The victim of rape is a powerful and frequently represented image in the canon of English literature. The evident, though ambiguous, pleasure of men in the idea of violated women speaks directly to the sexual anxiety and complexity of patriarchal politics. A woman who is raped becomes an object of sexual interest because she has had sexual 'knowledge' forced upon her. The possession of this knowledge removes her from the realm of virginity and chastity, makes her an active participant in male sexual experience. We may witness similar kinds of ambivalence in Shakespeare in the frequent presentation of the supplicating, kneeling woman, begging the powerful man to use his power in her behalf. The most memorably sexual such example is Isabella in *Measure for Measure* whose chaste kneeling arouses such sexual frenzy in Angelo. It would seem, then, that the chaste (and beautiful) woman in distress is enfolded into the bosom of patriarchy not because of her distress but because of her sexual potential.

Lavinia's body is the emblem of the evil of which the villains of the play are capable. It is also the emblem of the justifiable revenge her father seeks. To the villains she is reduced to an inarticulate fragment of humanity. Speechless and unable to communicate, she is the proof of the success of their destructive power. But they reckon without the human desire to speak and the male lust for vengeance, both of which urges are given iconic form in the play, most particularly in Titus's speech:

> Thou shalt not sigh, nor hold thy stumps to heaven,
> Nor wink, nor nod, nor kneel, nor make a sign,
> But I of these will wrest an alphabet,
> And by still practice learn to know thy meaning.
>
> (III,ii,43–5)

It is necessary that we remind ourselves that Lavinia does not speak after her rape. The men speak for her. Her silence is filled by male voices; it is not accepted by men as final or absolute. Her body and then her mind are invaded by males. The audience and her family receive only a male interpretation of her thoughts, but there is no available means of questioning that interpretation, so definitively do the men of the play dominate her. Even when she finally expresses herself, it is in a language and manner that is inevitably masculinist; Lavinia tells of the rape through the use of Ovid, and in Latin she describes her experience by writing it with a stick. The extent to which she is a subject of male domination is nowhere more eloquently exposed than here.

The carnage in the play, the almost natural resort to murder and violence as resolution argues a kind of intellectual crudeness which is not mitigated by reference to the classical sources of the drama.[9] And yet, of course, the blunt and incessant violence of the play is a way of restoring visible and palpable form to a multiplicity of ethical problems. The violence of the play functions somewhat like the lack of violence in *Richard II*. It supplies precise and iconographic definition to the actions by underscoring their political and cultural meanings. The language of *Titus* is all passionate and regularly stretched to the emotional limit. There is a fairly constant absence of modulation and ordinariness of expression, from the explosive opening fraught with rancour and strife to the last moments of Aaron's fury and Lucius's excoriation. The logical extension of this incessant passion is violence. Thus, resolution through brutality and killing is made part of a system of rational behaviour. The characters who participate in the volcanic actions of the play are themselves extreme types who exist on the edge of passion. They are centreless in the sense that they show no awareness of the ordinary and are driven by the highly charged conditions to the verge of passion; this passion is the only stable or constant feature of their lives. The typing, that is, is a necessary and inevitable feature of their presence. For their actions and emotions to even begin to seem logical the intensity must be immediately established. So the violent commencement of the play is immediately carried to an emotional extreme as two characters are viciously killed in the first scene.

The two leading female characters, Lavinia and Tamora, are functional, stereotypical opposites, standing on opposing margins of this man's world of love, death, and honour. As Lavinia is an emblem of chaste virtue, Tamora is the embodiment of sexual vice and cruelty. Between these two stand the glaring male antagonists, each side spurred on by the female figure who determines their direction and supplies the motive for their violent rage. The use of the female in this sense is one of the play's means of indicating the centrality of the female presence in the male world. For each side is determined to order the world according to the demands of the female figure at its heart. That Tamora is filled with hate and Lavinia with grief is no disincentive to the destructiveness of the men who fight for them. Lavinia's mangled body cries out for vengeance because vengeance is an ideologically determined and explicit resolution to its demand. Tamora too wants justice, though she carries her demand to the extremes of cruelty in her willingness to destroy the entire Andronicus family for the loss of the one son slain by Titus's command in the first scene. She swears:

> I'll find a day to massacre them all.
> And race their faction and their family,
> The cruel father, and his traitorous sons,
> To whom I sued for my dear son's life;
> And make them know what 'tis to let a queen

Kneel in the streets and beg for grace in vain.

(I,i,450–5)

She immerses herself in a lust for vengeance, bending every effort to its claims. But the revenge of Tamora, like that of Titus at the end, has an artistic form. It is planned in detail, given shape by invention, enjoyed sensually. And it falls most horribly on Lavinia as Tamora exhorts her sons to do the rape. In arguing that it is through Tamora and Lavinia that Titus himself is constructed, Douglas E. Green proposes that Tamora is made the more effective a revenger by her gender: 'Every desire she voices threatens Titus, Rome, and the patriarchal assumptions of the audience.'[10]

The dialogue between Tamora and Lavinia before the rape brings together the two female protagonists in an emblematic encounter which produces a social context for rape. Each woman refers to the male world as arbiter of that context. Each holds the same view of this kind of violence which is peculiarly that of man against woman. They share the recognition that rape is the one form of violence which places the woman beyond the pale of social recovery. Thus it is that Lavinia appeals to Tamora's womanliness, to that essential quality that binds them in kind if not in faith: 'O Tamora, thou bearest a womans face, – ' (II,iii,136). To Chiron she pleads, 'Do thou entreat her show a woman's pity' (147). But, as she loses hope of pity, Lavinia recurs to the world of men, to the dominant given of the play, the delicate difficulty of reconciling female sexual knowledge with social value. Only the love of men can give women position in the world. The loss of that love is worse than death:

> *Lavinia.* 'Tis present death I beg; and one thing more
> That womanhood denies my tongue to tell.
> O, keep me from their worse than killing lust,
> And tumble me into some loathesome pit,
> Where never man's eye may behold my body.
>
> (173–7)

Though Tamora initially acts out of a just grievance, the text condemns her by educing other crimes and criminal potentials, such as her illicit and 'unnatural' sexual liaison with Aaron the Moor. Thus her lust for revenge possesses the overtones of a frenetic sexual malevolence and quite expunges the element of right that the motive might supply. Green points out that Tamora's reminder that she herself once 'pour'd forth tears in vain' (II, 3, 163) 'cuts both ways: it establishes Titus' error as the source of Lavinia's plight, but it also transfers Titus' inhumanity to Tamora's unwomanly, "beastly" nature'.[11] In urging her sons to rape Lavinia, Tamora repudiates her 'womanhood' and allies herself with male lust. Lavinia's appeal to Tamora's womanliness proposes a deeper alliance than a merely political one. It argues a species of preconscious affinity shared by women, one which establishes their collective unity in opposition to men. Certainly the notion, deeply implicit in these lines, succeeds in serving a patriarchal model of womanliness, since it advances the notion of female complicity and 'special' female experience. Though it is no surprise that Tamora rejects this appeal, the play represents her rejection of it as a charged political moment when she effectively renounces her own sexual identity and identifies her desire with that of the male rapists. Indeed, Catherine Stimpson recognizes a lascivious quality in Tamora's encouragement of her sons to rape: 'Letting her boys "satisfy their lust" (II,iii,180) expresses her enjoyment of her sons' potency, which veers toward and approaches a sublimated incest.'[12] For all that, the inescapable fact of their sex binds Lavinia and Tamora in one common pursuit – the fear of male violence.

The ever likely prospect of male violence is one of the most deeply present cultural forms in the play. It determines the direction of events as no other idea or fact in the drama. It drives women together, however disparate and incompatible they may and can be. It is, to be sure, one of the hardiest ramifications of most modern cultures, and leads frequently to the misperception of women as a class. The fact is, however, in a play like this, women are bound together by their potential as victims. Indeed, it is just this common potential that forms the basis for Lavinia's plea to Tamora.

While the actual physical violence of *Titus Andronicus* is always committed by men, the men are often led to violence and assisted in violence by women. Tamora, like Lavinia, is a prisoner of her own body; she is physically weaker than the men she wishes to harm, as Lavinia, of course, is physically weaker than the men who harm her. Though some men are stronger than others, it is a given of *Titus Andronicus* that all women are weaker than all men. The fact creates and complicates the social and sexual culture of the play. In a drama of sexual difference, like this one, where every moment is dominated by allusion to the difference, where every conflict and every relationship is focussed on the fact of difference, the question of physical domination is absolutely crucial. So, as women are weaker than men, here they are outgunned by them on all fronts. Their motives are quite simply, from the early days of relative female innocence to the dreadful days of death, to get on with men and satisfy them. Their lives are centered on men, on dealing with them, pleasing them, and manipulating them. But nothing in their lives has form or relevance outside the determining worlds of men. The world of *Titus Andronicus,* violent and immoral, and overdetermined by codes of honour and villainy, is a Hell's Angels club. Women are used, abused, protected, maltreated etc., but always specifically as implements and agents of the stronger males they deal with. Their chance of survival in this maelstrom of violence is wholly contingent and dependent. This fact stands because they are physically helpless to change the essential point of their condition – their physical feebleness. One can assume that the value of women in predemocratic, preliberal, precapitalist societies has to do with their essential function in producing more men and more women to produce more men. The codes of honour, obligation, and protectiveness such as those reflected in *Titus* represent a 'civilizing' of the original and base motive of needing women. But a play like this, with its brutalization of the ethics of civilization leads inexorably back to the crude origins of these codes.

The sheer redundancy of women in all but a childbearing capacity is proposed by the speechless but sexually functional Lavinia and the purely wicked – i.e. socially useless – but fecund Tamora. Women are not a motive of honour and morality; they are an impediment to them. The glory of warfare and militarism is disoriented by women whose presence is a reproach to and corruption of male value. Their childbearing function is its own justification. The play strips away the layers of social and cultural value which have been systematically applied to this function as a way of giving ideological meaning to brutal necessity. When Tamora produces a visibly illegitimate child within the context of a socially sanctioned marriage, we are made to understand the true reason for Aaron's blackness. It is not some sophomoric black is evil, white is good ideology, but rather a dynamic dramatic means of revealing the deep and eternal – perhaps the inevitable – vulnerability of women within patriarchies. It may please the desire for justice to imagine Tamora meeting her deserts. More importantly, however, the evidence of Tamora's infidelity puts her out of the protection of the rational system by which she lives and brutalizes others. Suddenly, she is the victim not of male violence or male strength but of a *male law of nature* which has been produced by male societies to ensure their own perpetuation.

Aaron and Tamora's black infant is a symbol of great power in the play. Like Lavinia's, the baby's innocence, is a motive to terrible deeds of violence and murder. With the single exception of Aaron, all who see the child regard it as a hideous, and, in its blackness, a symbolic token of sexual villainy and unnaturalness. It proves what everyone has known all along – with the possible exception of Saturninus – that Tamora is a bad person. But no crime she commits in the play causes such universal outrage as her crime of being seen to have betrayed her husband. That chastity is a mainstay of patriarchy is nowhere more potently and vividly expressed in Shakespeare than in the vilifications which are heaped upon Tamora and her newborn baby.[13] Aaron's casual killing of the nurse imitates the highly formalized brutalism of other killings in the play.

The baby is a kind of symbolic counterpart to Lavinia. As a dramatic effect, its presence is a brilliant stroke. There, towards the conclusion of the worst carnage ever presented on stage, is the sudden appearance of a black baby. The reactions to the baby are spectacular. It is the merest of things, a 'tadpole' a 'toad', a creature that the best and worst characters would willingly kill – Lucius orders: 'A halter, soldiers, hang him on this tree, / And by his side his fruit of bastardy' (V,i,47–8). But it lives; in part this is because its father has the resources of cunning and courage to protect it, and the motive to preserve its life. He loves his child and the idea of himself that it contains. Nevertheless, the first emotion it inspires in those who see it, including its own mother, is violence. It must be killed. Like a woman, the child cannot survive without a protector. Like a woman it is a necessary nuisance. In this baby are concatenated the various cultural and social stigmas which are placed on the powerless. As a black child, in particular, it stands as a reminder of this masculine society's propensity to stratify all of its elements according to their capacity to command and enforce equality.

That the baby is a boy is all-important. As a male child it is invested with the chief value of males in patriarchal social groups like this one. The boy child can continue the paternal line as the woman cannot. The black boy child, because he is black, a stranger in this white world, provides something that a white child could not. He is definitive proof of the paternity of his black father. Despite the infidelity and promiscuity of his mother, the black child declares his paternity as no white child could in a white society. When the nurse shows the black baby to his father, there ensues a violent and passionate dialogue on the nature and function of colour in this culture. To Tamora, the Nurse, Chiron and Demetrius, the child must be killed because he is black and a defenseless baby – as women must be abused because they are defenseless. To Aaron his baby is the living proof of his own virility and the means whereby Aaron can live on beyond his own lifetime. He hankers, like the men in the play, for immortality. Aaron makes an eloquent and angry defense of blackness. The speech is well known. But why is it there at all? A thousand ways of continuing the drama without this violent and angry declamation exist, yet something prompted the author to produce a long speech on the virtues of blackness and the lifelessness of whiteness.

The language is potent and so muscularly embraces the mythologies of, most of all, black sexuality, that it could have been written by William Faulkner. Aaron starts with a denunciation of the white rapists, Chiron and Demetrius, and continues with a kind of celebration of the betterness of blackness:

> What, what, ye sanguine, shallow-hearted boys!
> Ye white-lim'd walls! ye alehouse painted signs!
> Coal-black is better than another hue
> In that it scorns to bear another hue,
> For all the water in the ocean
> Can never turn the swan's black legs to white
> Although she lave them hourly in the flood.
>
> (IV,ii,98–103)

The underdog in patriarchal societies, black men and white women in this case, is represented as, simply, a defective white man. Women – Lavinia and Tamora – and strange males – Aaron – are representative of the striving mass who sustain but are excluded from the structure of patriarchal authority. The women of the play and Aaron claim authority. They seem to wish white maleness on themselves. Tamora, of course resorts to a deviousness of impressive proportions to assert her will. She is not a man, she cannot say 'let it be as I decide' in the way that men can. She is compelled to use the devices that cultural convention assigns to women.

As those who fear his existence desire the death of Aaron's child, so those who wish to subdue women know that the resort to violence is the surest method of subduing women, of silencing them in the interest of patriarchal authority. To kill a baby is the easiest kind of murder. it involves the mere extinction of a still unjustified life. To kill or subdue a woman demands more of the killer. The woman is a socialized and developed human being with social alliances that put her into a realm of civilized existence which claims and demands social alliances beyond the command of an infant. Though an underdog, the woman is tied to the power structure in some way, even if only as a breeder of men. But her relation to it is always tentative because she is always capable of being physically subdued. Tamora almost acknowledges as much when, at the beginning of the play she looks for power through the means of marriage to the ruler. Without this marriage – or this political/power alliance – she is helpless. Women and children need men; they need marriage and they need family. Men have made and enforced this 'truth'. Without men, women and their children stand in danger of physical repression or violence.

Titus Andronicus, a play which embraces violence as way of life, is an exploration of the sensation of physical pain and the sensation of inflicting physical pain. It is also, of course, a study of the relation of male power and its subjects to physical pain. Ways of inflicting physical suffering on the self and others are provided here in amazing variety. But the play makes a distinction between hurting an enemy, and hurting an innocent. Hurting the innocent is represented as the most natural but the most brutal of acts. Titus's killing of his useless and tainted but innocent daughter is represented as an act of both hideous brutality and of the most palpable rationality. His suffering is greater than hers. Part of the attraction of violence is that it offers lasting resolutions to otherwise insoluble difficulties. And women are obvious and natural victims of violence within patriarchal structures, especially the intensely realized such structure as the Rome of this play. Where men dominate, and where domination is possible only through subduing others, the disaffected and subordinate men must find those weaker than themselves to fulfill the imperatives of the political and ideological structure within which they live. They find women and children whose physical inferiority makes them natural victims of the violent impulses nurtured in the patriarchal structure. The play, like the patriarchal culture which produces it, is a terrible wilderness where physical violence is simultaneously valorized and condemned. Titus's greatness rests, after all, on his capacity to kill. War – his arena of achievement, bloody and womanless – is the instrument and the manifestation of the violent means by which patriarchy establishes, maintains and enriches itself. Violence is the real gift that he brings home from the war. By violence he can hew down the stubborn forest of contradiction and resistance that the innocent and weak of his world put in his path. The logic of violence, which clearly determines that no problem is beyond being solved, offers men the fearful power of killing their own daughters in the larger interests of sustaining male supremacy.

7

The Killing of Cordelia

There are no final answers to the questions of why Cordelia must die or why Shakespeare decided to kill her off. This is not to say the critics have not tried to answer these questions. Literature and history abound with answers – answers theological, dramaturgical, philosophical, political, psychological. Lear knows, as readers and writers know, there is no answer to be got from asking the question. And yet the question of Cordelia's death arises inevitably, prompted as it is by the most moving and tragic spectacle the stage has to offer. Lear, in a physical action that mimics and equals in intensity the *pietas* of Michelangelo, wrenches the question from within himself. The answers that have been produced over the centuries eloquently, sometimes rhapsodically, indicate the ultimate futility of the pursuit of meaning through imaginative 'identification with' whatever has become valorized as meaningful. In the end, the critics are as perplexed and unsatisfied as Lear himself.[1] They know that they are moved by Lear's experience, but they find – we find – that the experience does not yield itself to rational analysis, and generations of audiences and readers have had to console themselves with the unsatisfying notion that the failure to find the reason for the suffering is the very basis of the tragedy.

While Cordelia's death and Lear's subsequent suffering are not in themselves explicable as meaningful individual experiences,[2] it is possible to examine them as rational consequences deriving from a systematically brutalizing structure whose inherent tendencies determine such tragic outcomes as these. To do so requires us to examine the political dimension that contextualizes the killing of Cordelia in terms of the sex and gender distortions which the play produces. Unlike the two other murdered heroines of Shakespearean tragedy, Lavinia and Desdemona, Cordelia is killed offstage and by a nameless soldier, a man she has not known and who has no better reason to kill her than that he is doing his job ('I cannot draw a cart nor eat dried oats;/ If it be man's work I'll

94

do't' [V,iii,39–40]). This soldier is then killed by a strangely and momentarily rejuvenated Lear who speaks of the event with a kind of boastful glee. 'Did I not, fellow?/ I have seen the day, with my good biting falchion / I would have made them skip' (V,iii,279–81).

The senseless and brutal killing of Cordelia offends all logic. As Desdemona and Lavinia's deaths are made to seem rational – if unjust – Cordelia is just another victim of the carnage around her. The war in which she and Lear are captured is a moral nightmare which produces genuine moral confusion. Cordelia and Lear are vanquished and Albany and Edgar are triumphant; yet they have always seemed to be on the same side. Lear himself becomes a victim of the same force of random destruction. Yet Lear has been an actor in this history, a real maker of events by misguided or merely unfortunate use of his considerable power. Thus his end belongs to a rational scheme on which the power-mongering within the world of the play depends. In a political structure like this one, where power is concentrated in few hands, where powerlessness is the lot of the many, the surrender of that power is a violation and betrayal of one of the chief values of that precise hierarchical structure. Power in Lear's world is designed to enable a social system of inequality. Inequality, indeed, is its dominant mode of survival and continuation. For some to have power, others must have no power. For only a few to have all the power, the many must have none. In such a system, how-ever, power is always tentative. For the system creates want as a condition of its own survival. That want, unfortunately for the possessors of power, is not produced solely among the poor. It is a condition of existence of *all* within the system. Though the poor may, in all innocence, only want bread, the rich and powerful are compelled by the overriding value of want to desire more wealth and more power. The greedy and grasping creatures of the play are not greedy and grasping because it is their natures to be so. The political structure that determines their existences also determines that they shall want as a condition of their being. And, of course, some, like Edmund, will go farther than others to satisfy a craving set into motion by an inherently unequal system which is entirely dependent upon inequality in power and wealth to survive.

Cordelia wants, but only in proportion to what she believes she deserves. This moderate desire establishes her oddness in the

drama. Lear, more perhaps than anyone, wants. He wants everything. In this he is the epitome of the value of want as a social practice by which the social formation renews itself. Desire – material,
sexual, and political – produces a kind of crazy vitality. Lear's sheer
and unmitigated greed for the love of his daughters, tied though
it may be to political conditions, is a brutish concatenation of the
function of desire in this world. And for two or three minutes he
is given what he craves, lavishly and unqualified, by Goneril and
Regan, the two daughters who understand – as their later behaviour
surely demonstrates – the nature and strength of their father's hunger for possession. Cordelia, in these terms, is the most subversive
character in the play. For her denial is not merely a reaction to the
king's unreasonableness. In her oddly conservative way she acts to
sabotage a world by claims that are consonant with patriarchy. But
the *Lear* world is one in which patriarchy has extended itself to a
logical but dangerous limit. The hunger for power overrides every
other consideration amongst those who have it or want it. It is to
this excess that Cordelia addresses her energy initially. She is not
merely saying no to the demand of her father; rather she is saying
no to an entire society whose life is predicated upon the instilled
drive to want.

Cordelia repudiates a dominant social ethic. The society of *King
Lear* coheres by virtue of the practice of desire. It is a force by
which patriarchal authority is maintained. What we see in the
familial structures of the play are structures whose survival
directly addresses the highly valorized ethic of possessiveness. The
embedded practice of patrilineal possession and inheritance, hedged
as it is with legal and traditional safeguards, betrays anxiety about
the evident or potential impulse to disrupt that lineage, to shatter the
smooth transition of power and wealth that we are led to anticipate,
for example, in Gloucester's family. Or that we see alluded to in
the families of Lear's married daughters.[3] Edmund is a usurper of
wealth and power, much like Bolingbroke in *Richard II*, but he is
not a threat to the structure under which it is legally obtainable,
as Bolingbroke and the other would-be kings of the histories also
do not threaten the political structure – a point that has been
argued in the first chapter. Cordelia, far more radically subverts,
or, rather, threatens, the entire political schema by which patrilineal
succession and its adherent policies survive. As an affronted woman
Cordelia must confront the Lear world with a posture and voice
that defy patriarchy in terms which expose its frailty. Jonathan

Goldberg points out that Cordelia's power lies in her refusal of construction by males – 'the demand that her silence represents, a resistance to the end of the megalomaniac acquisitiveness marked in Lear's attempt to appropriate everything, even her death. Her silence resists his speech . . . His final negations are more finely tuned to her silence, a submission at last to the limits of utterance.'[4] In a sense, Cordelia performs the ultimately subversive act by her silence: she uses patriarchy against itself by using the patriarchal ideal of the silent woman (discussed in Chapter 6), that icon of chastity and submission, as the way of defying patriarchy. Cordelia's 'nothing' or silence is, like female sexuality itself, her own secret, private retreat, beyond the reach of patriarchal intervention.

The Lear world cannot survive if the ethical and political stances of Cordelia are to obtain dominance. An essential political practice of the men of power in *Lear* is the production of evidence of power. Thus the wealth of the titled participants of the first scene has real rhetorical force. And, notwithstanding the Peter Brook *King Lear*, which tended to equalize and democratize the characters in a shared world of hardship and poverty, the text adamantly insists on the differences between rich and poor, men and women, on the artificiality of those differences and on their origins in ideology and the politics of power. Cordelia, like Lear, is caught by the wish to recover nature in its pristine form. But nature has become so overlaid with politics as to be beyond recovery. It has become yet another, crucial ideological form appropriated and defined by authority. Thus, every allusion in the play to nature is suspect, and revelatory more of a hopelessly unachievable condition than a measurable state of being.

Lear's 'Which of you shall we say doth love us most,/ That we our largest bounty may extend/ Where nature may with merit challenge?' (I,i,52–3) is an utterly rational question posited within a rationalized social structure. Indeed, the question epitomizes the structure of the power-possession equivalence in a world where love is understood to be synonymous with power. There is a kind of defiant audacity in Lear's question since it asks the daughters to give words to the credo by which everyone present appears to have lived without always acknowledging the fact. The question and the love contest it provokes have produced a great deal of critical anxiety which has revealed itself in mainly moral explanations of the blatant immorality of the question itself. And yet, the question logically, if combatively, addresses the evident collusion of all present in a systemic acquisitiveness by which the classes present onstage are sustained. We may assume the presence of some servants or attendants, and certainly an aristocracy carefully ranked.⁵ Lear is, in short, demanding a public affirmation of a way of life from his daughters and collaboration from his subjects who, except for Kent, stand passively by while the performance is played out. Indeed, the stunning silence of all the nobles but Kent, as their monarch acts to banish his truest daughter, does not argue cowardice on their parts. Nothing any of them does later in the play suggests that *they* fear authority. Gloucester and Albany's silence on the subject of the banishment of Cordelia and Kent argues only a tacit support of patriarchal monarchy in its confrontation with subversion. The other noblemen present may be said, even at this early stage, to harbour designs on Lear's power and property. But they all have one thing in common that Cordelia's challenge threatens: they all have a profound interest in the maintenance of the patriarchal system. They all have or expect to have heirs (Goneril's 'child of spleen' is clearly a thing of the future) through whom to maintain and hold power and wealth. In this sense, then, they must all unite against the ideology implied in Cordelia's denial of her father's wishes.

What Cordelia will not accept is the conditions of Lear's oath. But more important, she will not accept Lear's right to make her take the oath. Her famous 'Nothing' is a violently reductive challenge to Lear's and everyone else's conception of hierarchical authority. As a response to the powerful and seductive invitation it is a shocking repudiation of the entire process and that very ideology which sets it in motion. Cordelia declares war on the patriarchal politics that insists on reproducing itself in ceremonies such as these whose purpose is to assert the dominance of patriarchal might. For this reason, no nobles with heirs can side with Cordelia and Kent; to do so is to endorse a dangerous revolt against the very power that makes and keeps them nobles. Kent seems to be familyless, isolated and alone, willing to invest his power in the service of his beloved King and Cordelia. This lonely independence releases him, as it does no other noble, from the concerns and bonds of power and property. To such a state Cordelia must reduce herself to resist the force of political oppression.

For her to have accepted her father's conditions, she would have had to accept bondage to the fact and practice of oppression. That, surely, is the meaning of the love contest; to bind the daughters

in a publicly declared and socially approved and validated subservience to the method of politics that ensures their submission.
Goneril and Regan who are securely married are already, when the
play begins, a part of the system of patriarchal oppression. Their
individual accommodations with that system are revealed in the
domestic scenes involving them. Their putative subservience to
their husbands and their desire for Edmund's love indicate that
they are decidedly a part of the machinery of patriarchism and
that conformity to its politics will be their means of advancement.
Their lies about their love of Lear are logical products of the
system itself, where lying ensures success while truth exposes the
contradictions with which the system is fraught. Indeed, the entire
first scene is predicated upon lies and distortions and half-truths.
From Gloucester's crude, macho references to Edmund's mother,
to Lear's monstrous lies about the precise and exact division of
the kingdom into three equal parts, to Goneril and Regan's lies
about their love of the king, the lies mount grossly. Lying, we
see is a condition of social intercourse in this world. Its long
and practiced use is indicated by the readiness with which it is
produced, by the way in which it is supported as a practice. For
it has a potent strength as the chief means of concealing the very
things that may threaten the order under which the *Lear* world
functions.

Cordelia is a virgin, a member of only one household. She has not
yet been required to do as her sisters have done and divide herself
according to the dictates of patriarchy. Such division, naturally,
weakens the woman. We note how Cordelia sees her use of her
love: 'when I shall wed,/ That lord whose hand must take my
plight shall carry/ Half my love with him, half my care and
duty' (I,i,100–102). It is a giving, selfless love, a love that leaves
nothing for herself. What alarms Lear in Cordelia's statement is its
repudiation of the hierarchical individualism for which Lear stands.
Rather than being, as Lawrence Danson has argued, an expression
of traditional values,[6] Cordelia's 'bond' is a repudiation. Cordelia
recognizes no 'natural' authority. She acknowledges instead – and
more wisely and subversively – social and political obligation, *determined* patterns of affection which have more to do with politics than
'natural' bonds. Her debt of love to her husband is *equal*, she says, to
that to her father. Tacitly the statement acknowledges the primacy of
men in a tough world, but it declares the patent artificiality of their
dominance, as it seeks to restore an evidently unused structure of

allegiance. The two men in this speech to whom she allows the debt of love are impersonal and general; they are 'husband' and 'father', not Lear and France or Burgundy. Indeed, the fact that she makes the speech before she knows who is to *be* her husband, indicates the purely theoretical quality of the love she is setting aside for him. The drama makes nothing seem more natural. Cordelia is about to be given away in marriage to a king or a duke; in other words to a man who will maintain her. Who he is of secondary importance. He *is* his function. He protects princesses. As it turns out the duke protects princesses for a high price while the king of France protects them in exchange for no higher a price than their love and the proprietorship of their virtues. Burgundy, who obviously has precedence over France, is repelled by Cordelia's new state, for it separates patriarchal matrimony from wealth; it proposes the unthinkable notion of a woman's human value in and of itself, untied to property. Such a notion strikes at the heart of the kind of political structure upon which the premises of this monarchy stand. France declares himself an enemy to the English monarchy by his willingness to take Cordelia, 'dowerless' and 'thrown to [his] chance' (I,i,258). Cordelia and France in their actions of refusal and revulsion offer a challenge to the order of the court in proposing another order. An oppositional stance that is destroyed in the war, but one whose presence intensifies the dangerous multiplicity of the text.

Gloucester's shock, when he next appears, muttering to Edmund, contains not a single word about Cordelia, the banishment of whom is the most vivid event of the first scene. The absence of Cordelia from his litany of things gone wrong is significant. Has she so soon been erased from the kingdom, so soon from the scene of banishment. He puzzles:

> Kent banished thus? And France in choler parted?
> And the King gone tonight? Prescribed his power,
> Confined it to exhibition? All this done
> Upon the gad! Edmund, how now? What news?
>
> (I,ii,23–6)

Six questions in four lines. Concentrated bemusement about the outcome of recent events. Yet Cordelia's powerful disabling of the machinery of patriarchy goes unmentioned, though her new husband's ire is a source of worry. It is a world where the actions and desires of powerful men matter; where maids have not even sufficient presence to disturb – or who, if they disturb are more safely forgotten at once. At least that is how Cordelia's explosive honesty would seem to have affected Gloucester. Gloucester's world is determined more specifically than Lear's by the tangible, the political, the power-centered. He is a less sensitive and less narcissistic version of his king. He pursues the relation of cause and effect relentlessly and consistently – as patriarchy has taught him to do. He is, potentially, a better politician (or manager of power, in this play's terms) than Lear, being more given to rationality and more reliant on evidence; though, obviously, he is vulnerable in these areas as well. Lear is more given to emotionality and impulsiveness, less interested in why things happen than in that they happen.

It is these characteristics that make Lear so vulnerable to the subversive and rational questioning of Cordelia. His world is a fragile place, its structures of stability and order are easily upset because he is driven by a sense that they are unfixed. This conviction is what leads him to assert their fixedness so passionately and forcefully and self-destructively. The love contest is merely a means of restabilizing the system of hierarchical monarchy by which he has lived. It is, after all, only Lear among the court who perceives the tragic failures of power in his England, its creation of and seduction by rampant individualism. Jonathan Dollimore has written: 'For Lear dispossession and displacement entail not redemptive suffering but a kind of suffering recognition . . . . [He] does acknowledge blame.'[7] Cordelia the dispossessed princess becomes a part of that substratum in Lear's world; she is one of those whose existence on the margins is discovered so stunningly by a half-crazed king. Cordelia's rejection of Lear's request for unqualified love derives from the kind of recognition that only one who belongs among the weak could provide. While she does not aim to destroy the power structure, she knows she must change one master for another, a father for a husband. In her answer she indicates a desire to maintain ties with both. Her sisters by their cruel assertiveness and ruthless dishonesty defy the limits that culture places upon their gender. They cast their lots in with the men they are tied to in order to overcome such paternalistic obstacles as the love-contest. Yet it is that very ritual of publicity that indicates their acceptance of the stipulations of the gender roles that the patriarchy supplies. Part of the reason that Cordelia has been so loved by an order-orientated

criticism is that she has been seen to recover and reaffirm in a more
Christian and loving way the hierarchical patterns that are almost
overturned by her even more dangerous and subversive father.
When Lear recovers from madness Cordelia is there to revivify
the bonds that are called 'natural'. She still is a perfect daughter
without having to give up the point she makes in the first scene.
The immaculate daughterliness of Cordelia is best captured in the
passionately imagined act of 'O! look upon me, Sir,/ And hold your
hand in benediction o'er me' (IV,vii,57–8). Of course, anyone must
have a heart of granite not to be moved by this display of filial
love, but we may note that the form the display takes is clearly in
keeping with the structure of patriarchal discourse (in word and
gesture) on which the politics of the play is based and which has
caused such terrible upheaval. And yet, as Dollimore cautions, 'To
see her death as *intrinsically* redemptive is simply to mystify both
her and death.'[8]

After the battle near Dover, Cordelia comes back into her own
as a force in the play. Defeated, she is nevertheless reunited to
her father who has been turned inside out by physical and mental
suffering. To Lear, the world has exposed its gross underbelly. His
madness has spewed forth in powerful and disturbing recognitions
which have made terrible havoc of the steady patriarchal order by
which the court protects itself from its own political and social
iniquity. In his maddest moments Lear is clearest about the fearful
contradictions of his world. He sees and comprehends them in all
their sadness and filth; the use and abuse of women, the horror
of poverty, and the ways in which he and his court manage not
to recognize such violent, endemic and casual cruelty which has
been conveniently built into the system of maintaining power. The
experience of poverty has made him know that the poor are poor,
that he has taken too little care of this. We have seen in discussing
Prince Hal and the nature of monarchical power in England, that 'its
moral authority rests upon a hypocrisy so deep that the hypocrites
themselves believe it'.[9] Lear has not shown the brilliance of Hal,
has not known that to be a successful king he has needed to be
a kingly hypocrite. Unprotected by the carapace of insensitivity
that such knowledge demands and implies, he has had to find
out the hard way what the likes of Hal have always known.
And the hard way has almost destroyed him. He has discovered
the hypocrisy and cruelty of the structure and systems that once
sustained him:

> There thou might'st behold
> The great image of Authority:
> A dog's obey'd in office.
> Thou rascal beadle, hold thy bloody hand!
> Why dost thou lash that whore? Strip thine own back;
> Thou hotly lusts to use her in that kind
> For which thou whipp'st her. The usurer hangs the
>   cozener.
> Thorough tatter'd clothes small vices do appear.
>
> (IV, vi, 155–63)

The unhinging recognitions about sexuality hinted at in these lines and piercingly felt elsewhere by the king have a different cast for the women of the play. Lear's revulsion against sexuality stems from loathing and fear of women, but its stimulus is less apparent than its presence. His language chokes with malevolent images of the designs of women against men, with representations of women as horrible, stinking, serpentine sexual beings who severely threaten men. Obsessed as he is with deception, he recognizes women as the arch deceivers. Their sex is their secret, and nothing he can say or know will ferret out the truth of that secret, which is, of course, that ultimately, women's sexual practice is innately undetectable, private. Lear can look at Poor Tom and feel compassion.[10] As he does so, the play propels the poor into a bright public glare, it invites us to acknowledge them as the monarch has done. Lear recalls women – his daughters, a simpering dame, whores. And he hates them all. There is no compassion left. Women are his enemy, demonized and reduced to their sexual and reproductive function.

> Down from the waist they are Centaurs,
> Though women all above:
> But to the girdle do the Gods inherit,
> Beneath is all the fiend's: there's hell, there's
>   darkness
> There is the sulphurous pit – burning, scalding,
> Stench, consumption.
>
> (IV,vi,122–7)

There is surely no need to avoid the assumption that the dark sulphurous pit for Lear is the vagina. The misogyny of the King at this point in the play seems to derive from a specific hatred of

Goneril and Regan. But the hatred takes a crazy form as it seems to find expression in fury against female sexuality as though it were the cause of his pain. Lear does not distinguish Cordelia from this mass of womankind whom he believes have brought him to this pass. It takes the Gentleman to remind him that 'Thou hast one daughter,/ Who redeems nature from the general curse/ Which twain have brought her to' (IV,vi,202–4). Lear, characteristically, does not acknowledge the reminder, but goes on and on in his careering anguish. 'The misogyny of King Lear, both the play and its hero,' writes Kathleen McLuskie, 'is constructed out of an ascetic tradition which presents women as the source of the primal sin of lust, combining with concerns about the threat to the family posed by female insubordination.'[11]

But what of Cordelia? Where does she fit into this highly complicated structure of patriarchal power? Her sisters have succeeded in subverting the power of the King, their father; their conspiracy against him is contingent upon the presence and maintenance of a patriarchal authority and their desire to replace his monarchical power with their own. On this substitution all involved in the expulsion of the king depend. The king must be destroyed so that his position and power may be reassigned. Cordelia's 'bond' and her marriage to France have put her outside this pale of self-interest. Her return in arms against the united English powers threatens to dislocate the power-possession axis. As a banished exile, she is perceived as a known subversive who tries to wrest the government from those who possess it. Their interests are so firmly entrenched, so flagrantly a perpetuation of the patriarchal order, that any alternative to themselves is a danger. Cordelia, like many a political exile, enjoys some support within England, even after she has left. Her feeling for the helpless and defenseless king extends itself.

The Fool's reaction to her absence speaks of a Cordelia who felt kinship with the powerless: he is one of the most wretched of the drama, belonging to no class, living always in fear of whipping and abuse. His love for Cordelia carries her to his level, indicates her repudiation of the values that make him so powerless and expendable. It is, in part, the Fool's love of and loyalty to Cordelia that shows her dangerousness. A gap between them has been bridged, though we never know how much or for how long. Yet, in closing the gap between Court and dependant, Cordelia has broken a covenant of her class. She has shown the possibility of closing the gulf between rich and poor. It is interesting that Lear, until his 'In boy; go first. You houseless poverty' (III,iv,26), appears to regard the various breaches between the powerful and the powerless as part of a 'natural' order, as a divinely ordained structure which admits of no alteration. During his experience of poverty – an experience as Dollimore notes from which he has always been protected[12] – he perceives the possibility of a more humane world of shared experience:

> Take physic, Pomp;
> Expose thyself to feel what wretches feel,
> That thou mayst shake the superflux to them
> And show the Heavens more just.
>
> (III,iv,32–6)

The last two words are a remarkable concession. They adumbrate a juster world than that in which it is possible to demand and quantify love. The words 'more just' link Lear and Cordelia in a common pursuit of a different world: to this pursuit Lear has come late and through hardship, but at the moment when he says these words he is a passionate believer in a society where the want of necessities is a common rather than a rare experience. Cordelia proves her commitment to her love by raising an army and attacking the forces of the British patriarchy. She is a revolutionary hero of an ancient time who risks – and gives – her life in the cause of love:

> No blown ambition doth our arms incite,
> But love, dear love, and our ag'd father's right.
>
> (IV,iv,27–8)

What exactly is 'our ag'd father's right'? Is it the monarchical power which he enjoyed before he gave it away? Is it the purely paternal right to retire in peace and crawl 'unburthen'd' towards death? If the former, then, for all the modesty of Cordelia's claims, she is here to overthrow by force a legally constituted power. For the division of the kingdom was a legitimate political act within the power of the monarch who made it. In its war against the invading French army, some strange bedfellows are made, not least Edgar fighting on the side of Edmund, or Albany on the side of Regan and Goneril. Clearly, in the minds of all the English forces, Cordelia is a threat to national stability and safety and must be vanquished for it to be preserved. Cordelia comes, one way or another, to assume power in England, to destroy the present shared dukedom that it has become. Even if her motive is only to supply to the king the power of living out the rest of his days peaceably in England, she comes to England to assert *her* will there. Is it worth noting that her aggressive intention is partly indicated by the simple fact that she does not rescue Lear when she can and return with him to France? She comes to overthrow what looks like an evil regime and to replace it with something else whose nature and politics she will determine. And this, in an important sense, is why she must die.

It has often been noted of Edmund that, though a bad piece of work, he is quite astute and clever. Yet he orders the secret murders of Lear and Cordelia. It seems likely that he recognizes in them, even in their captivity, a political threat to his own apparently realizable ambitions for greater power. By acting to have them killed he is assuming the reins of power, is acting autonomously, and wresting from his opponents the power of restoring them. As captives, Cordelia and Lear supply a new perspective on the Court, a knowledge of its weakness. Lear's 'Come, let's away to prison' speech proposes a Court whose life is entirely frivolous, dishonest, grotesque. His relish for prison produces in his imagination and out of his pain a Court that is a prison and a prison that is a kind of idealized Court. Lear sees prison as the possibility of retreat and removal from this world. To Coppelia Kahn, in this speech, where Lear imagines their life in prison, he 'transcends the rigid structure of command and obedience that once framed his world . . . Parent and child are equal, the gestures of deference that ordinarily denote patriarchal authority now transformed into signs of reciprocal love.'[13] The moment is of a piece, in political importance, with Lear's recognitions on the heath, for it surely suggests the subversive idea that reciprocal, equal love is contrary to the interests of patriarchy. In her heroic wish to 'see these daughters and these sisters' (V,iii,7), Cordelia expresses a desire for meaning and for coming to terms with the history and politics of her family, even in the face of death. And this is part of her danger to the state; her refusal to fear the present and the materially real. As her father desires escape, Cordelia demands confrontation.

Cordelia's motive, from her first words, 'What shall Cordelia speak? Love and be silent' (I,i,61), is a politics of opposition. She rejects authority that insists on its authority. Banished, she returns, not unlike Bolingbroke, to impose her will on the new authority, to usurp its power. For there is nothing so perilous or impossible, as Bolingbroke and Cordelia have to learn, as a half of a revolution, one that does not complete its cycle. There is no way of taking power from those in power without taking all of that power. For them to concede some power is the same as their conceding all their power. Though the terms of good and evil clearly operate in Cordelia's revolution as motives for heroic, life-endangering action, the translation of moral motives into action takes the form of careful policy. Cordelia's presence is in itself a reproach to her sisters. She marches into England at the head of the army of France for a principle of moral order and right. Her attempt to rescue Lear is only a part of her enterprise; for to rescue Lear fully, she must restore him to his throne and give back to him the world and the self he gave away. The play subtly and dangerously proposes some of the huge political difficulties and the need for definitive choices that we have encountered in the English histories, especially in *Richard II*. It suggests the always unanswered question of good usurper versus bad king in a new and complex way. For it insists on Cordelia as an invader by posing Albany against her invasion; by having Edgar wish Albany well in the battle against Cordelia with, 'Fortune love you!' (V,i,46) That arrangement of benign force against Cordelia makes her defeat a matter of greater interest and uncertainty than is generally acknowledged. Cordelia knows, as her armed presence indicates, that her 'ag'd father's right' is more than just a domestic, paternal function; that it is inseparable from his political right. The political structures of monarchy, especially a monarchy that is so hedged with and dependent on divinity and mystery for its support and maintenance, tend to fix identity and the relationship of the individual to the polity, as Lear is fixed as king; and, indeed, a vast deal of creative energy goes into reaffirming Lear's kingliness in lines that are very well known. Cordelia's 'How does my royal Lord? How fares your Majesty?' (IV,vii,44) eloquently declares her stance.

Cordelia's death, which is made to seem so random, unnecessary and, even, casual, is in fact a recognition of and a response to the danger that she is. Her killing is a definitive political act, not the triumph of malevolence or evil, but a necessity in this struggle which she has entered and whose stakes are so high. They are not merely – though they do include – the substitution of one kind of rule for another, they are the values of entrenched individualism protecting themselves against change. And it is Cordelia, in this material and vicious world, with her army and her friends in Britain, who truly makes the change seem possible. There is no place, no politics, no ideological system that can make Cordelia safe in Britain again. There is no way that she can be accommodated to live with the likes even of Edgar and Albany after her attempt to destroy the very basis of their values. Her attack on Britain must be interpreted by the power axis that governs as an attack on the state. Her claim to be rescuing her father is belied by the considerable might she brings with her and by the fearful response of the British powers. By leading an advancing army, Cordelia has brought subversion out into the open, into a last stage where it confronts the forces it would destroy. Cordelia's revolutionary potential – her capacity, that is, for entirely transforming the polity and the state – is carried to the brink of fulfillment. The entire political leadership has had to look into the face of political upheaval and transformation. Cordelia and her father are ordered killed by a knowing and experienced victor. Edmund's is a rational manner of dealing with genuine peril.

That Cordelia is a woman is a looming fact of this play. The part she usurps is the usually male part of rescuer and rectifier. She is, after all, a woman warrior of heroic ambition. That a woman is threatening the stability of the state and that this woman is brutally hanged and her dead body is carried into the last political forum that play provides are all events that affirm and deny conventional assumptions about her sex. Coppelia Kahn usefully reminds us that 'at the end of *King Lear* only men are left'.[14] On the one hand, the image of Cordelia's body in Lear's arms is a visible reiteration of her physical slightness and 'femininity'; in the reader's imagination and in performance Lear must be able to bear this dead weight of his daughter. This image endorses a political code that insists on the natural bonds of parent and child, father and daughter. The alternate image of Cordelia at the head of an invading army, challenges this image of 'femininity', offering instead a muscular riposte to the equally muscular Goneril and Regan. Cordelia, dead, can also reify the value of her failed revolution. The feeble, staggering king is more than an erring father; he is his nation trammeled by an oppressive patriarchy and ultimately beyond rescue. It is such images of the play that insist on being located within the theoretical frameworks with which we surround them. On this level, it can surely be argued that the reason she dies is forcibly and definitively to validate a structure of nature and kinship that patriarchy has consolidated as its own. The gloomy last moments and closing speeches of the play bring us back to the unpalatable reality of the apparent indominability of patriarchy. For, as Dollimore has noted, the political conditions at the close of the play are such as obtained in the beginning; a world of wealth and poverty, of power and powerlessness is reconstituted despite the devastations of murder, execution, death, and war.[15]

8

The Murder of Desdemona

The reason that Desdemona must die is presented quite straightforwardly. To Othello she must die 'else she'll betray more men'. To us the cause is possibly less clear than it is to Othello, but we tend to agree, as we do not in the case of Cordelia, that it is based on a rational system in which patrilineal succession and patriarchal authority are the cornerstones of the social process. That process, in spite of itself and its male dominance, is ultimately dependent upon female sexual fidelity which, therefore, becomes the chief value of the entire social structure. It is the stability of this very patriarchal society that Othello is committed to protecting, though he must kill his wife to do it. His stand for patriarchy is, however, also a barely disguised act of revenge for sexual betrayal; the political and the personal coalesce with particular force in cases of sexual misprision. To address the murder of Desdemona it is necessary to consider the political implications of the killing of a woman as an act and a means of restabilizing and reifying a social order that is contingent on dominance and submission. The method of the killing of Desdemona has a special resonance in Shakespeare. Of the three murders of heroic women, this one is the most protracted, detailed, minutely observed. The lingering slowness of the killing and the preoccupation of the play with its method and circumstances are what make it fascinatingly different from the examples of Lavinia and Cordelia, whose deaths are respectively sudden and offstage.

The coincidence of violence and patriarchal ideology is a factor in the murder of all three heroines. In each case, though less obviously in the case of *Lear*, the heroine's murder follows from a male desire to deny her autonomy. In each case patriarchy constructs women as actual or potential adversaries who need to be subdued. And, finally, in each case, the killer assumes a male *right* to kill a woman. Almost never in a Shakespeare play does a woman kill a man, nor does any woman argue her right to kill a man. But in the three tragedies in which women are murdered by men, the right of the man to kill the woman is asserted and acted upon. Killing begins to seem in these assertions of right, a consistent – though obviously extreme – extension of patriarchal rights. The frantic individualism that is released in the tragedies takes its most vicious but logical form in the right to kill the other who stands between the individual and his realization of his individuality. That individuality, in the case of *Othello*, is utterly bound up with the woman's individuality being absorbed and entrapped within his own. Othello does, indeed, kill Desdemona for a cause, an idea. That idea, endorsed by every male in the play, is that the woman has no right to an autonomous, separate existence. This is a belief that is central to the ways in which Desdemona's running away from her father is seen, the way in which her marriage is seen, the way in which her 'infidelity' is seen by every character in the play except Emilia. The play's villains and heroes alike perceive the possibility of female separateness as an affront to all males and a violation of a sacred canon of the paternal/patriarchal relations by which they retain social balance.

The beginning of *Othello* includes the presentation of a remarkable instance of the 'bonding' of men in opposition to a woman. When Brabantio becomes aware of Desdemona's elopement, or bid for freedom, he begins to confide in and seek solace from Roderigo himself, the man whom he had been reviling moments before. Now he asks Brabantio for confirmation of his fears and suspicions:

> is there not charms,
> By which the property of youth and maidhood
> May be abus'd? Have you not read, Roderigo,
> Of some such thing?
>
> (I,i,171–4)

The new friendship, based upon a mutual animosity towards a female quite as much as towards a male 'other', comes to a resounding climax with Brabantio's declaration to Roderigo: 'O that you had her!' (176) The motive for all of this anxiety is racial hatred, a disposition shared by all of the other characters of the play and, as Karen Newman has trenchantly shown, by a huge majority of the influential critics.[1] More importantly, perhaps, Newman notes the way in which the patriarchal white society ties the 'monstrous' black man and the woman together in a constructed complicity against itself: 'Both Othello and Desdemona deviate from the norms of the sex/race system in which they participate from the margins.'[2]

Brabantio's immediate response to his daughter's flight is to resort to violent means to retrieve her. He urges, 'call up all my people' (141), 'Raise all my kindred', (168) 'Call up my brother' (176), implying with each summons the need of physical force to restore order to his existence. This confluence and interdependence of violence and order is a constant element of the patriarchal structure of *Othello*. Law is the resort of civil disagreement, but to resolve the question of proprietorial right Venetians like Brabantio use the sword. Thus it is that he attempts to challenge the Moor and retrieve his daughter in the streets of Venice. Thus it is when Othello sees himself as having lost a proprietorial power over Desdemona that he too resorts to violence; and Iago, when he fears that Emilia's assertion of autonomy has gone too far, also uses violence to subdue and silence her. Patriarchal rights must be protected at any cost, even at the cost of the woman's life.

The process of socially embedded violence leading to violence against women – Desdemona and Emilia – continues. For all that 'this is Venice, / My house is not a grange' (105–6), it is Brabantio who readies himself to retrieve his daughter by violent means and prepares violently to attack Othello. He and his followers draw swords as he cries 'Down with him, thief!' (I,ii,57) Othello declines to fight and the confrontation continues in the senate chamber before the Duke. Violence includes the intention to compel another person into physical, emotional, or intellectual submission, and if submission is not possible, to bring about their incapacity to continue resistance by maiming or death. A political structure that is so dependent upon authority and obedience, upon the identification of its elements and component parts as categories, absolutely requires the means of maintaining these categories. If, concomitantly, the elements of the social formation are required to be obedient and subordinate to an individual rather than a collective authority, then the means of maintaining that obedience must belong to the individual authority in question. In *Othello*, Othello and Desdemona, as members of subordinate elements of the hierarchical society that is called Venice, necessarily are answerable to the power of Duke, Senators, father and husband. In the domestic sphere of father and husband, violence assumes a different form from that it takes in the political arena. Where political authorities use violence to subdue political foes and (if there is a distinction) criminals through the impersonal agency of the army or the policing authority, fathers and husbands are themselves violent so as to control individuals who live under their legally constituted sway – in this case daughter and wives. The distinction of course is what enables violence in the domestic sphere where, typically, men are violent towards women because women are made 'naturally' subservient to them by virtue of their normal – though not invariable – physical inferiority. Desdemona and Emilia do not try to hurt or kill their husbands because, in part, they are physically not capable of doing so and, in part, because they are women who seem not to be schooled in the male social practice of control. Carol Thomas Neely writes of the women of *Othello* that they are 'not murderous, and they are not foolishly idealistic or foolishly cynical as the men are . . . they combine realism with romance, mockery with affection'.[3]

The scene in the senate establishes the basis for the violent outcome of the marriage of Othello and Desdemona. There, in the presence of the highest representative of the law of Venice, the pecking order of control, dominance, and submission is assessed and determined. The entire scene is a conscious, deliberate scrutiny of the nature and extent of the power of individuals over other individuals. It cannily imbricates into the examination a global political difficulty having to do with the domination of the people of Cyprus and the contingent need to maintain the subjection of these people with the help of the Moor. In other words each discussion of power – the personal and the political – invades the other, so that no decision is independent. The need of Othello in Cyprus has the potential to influence the decision about Othello's right to Desdemona. Thus the extent to which Desdemona's declaration of a divided duty determines the outcome is never clarified: the political is firmly implied in the Duke's decision.

The Duke's initial promise to Brabantio confirms the presence of violence in the process:

> Whoe'er he be, that in this foul proceeding
> Hath thus beguil'd your daughter of herself,
> And you of her, the bloody book of law
> You shall yourself read

(I,iii,65–8)

'your daughter of herself, / And you of her' propounds a line of dependencies of familial and patriarchal relationships that suggest the authoritative structure as a 'natural' one. Perhaps most interesting here is the relationship of daughter to (her)self: that is, the functioning social persona determined *as* the self. It is this socially determined identity that Desdemona repudiates. That she is a daughter, of course she does not deny, but that her self and her daughterliness are inseparable and indissoluble she rejects as the ideology of a society that means to subject her to itself. She says in replying to her father's demand for obedience 'I challenge, that I may profess' (I,iii,188).

An inherent social contradiction is normally resolved as daughter becomes wife by the ritual of marriage, by a switching of identities. This elopement is another serious and consequential example of the broken ritual in Shakespeare. Its violent avoidance of the normally smooth movement between states of femaleness gives the lie to the entire process of exchanging identity, proving that it *can* be done without social sanction and ritual. The turmoil that ensues from such events as this elopement is society's way of fighting back, of demonstrating that its need has priority over that of the individual. In this curious fashion, Iago becomes the tool of Venetian authority in proving the folly of challenging society's rules and ways. And, indeed, as is well known, there is a potent tradition going all the way back to Thomas Rhymer and including T. S. Eliot, that chooses to see the play as precisely this kind of lesson: that is that the play is 'a warning to all good Wives that they look well to their Linnen'.[4] Iago is society's (our's, theirs?) avenging angel who destroys those who challenge its canons; he threatens to turn the drama into a reactionary morality play.

Iago, indeed, does talk on behalf of the world of order and rational structure; such argument being the chief of his means of penetrating the defenses of Othello. It is he, after all, who whispers demonically into Othello's ear of the way in which the codes of Venice – and by implication all European society – are challenged by this unnatural marriage of black and white. He is a conduit from Venice to Othello, interpreting and dictating the ways of the white society that Othello has so proudly and dramatically invaded.[5] It is he who identifies the problem and he who knows the violent solution. It is Iago who supplies the rationale by which the whole process of sexual infidelity leads to murder. Iago shows Othello that the way he has chosen – that is, the way of passion – is reasonable, precedented, and even ethical.

The first threat of violence against Desdemona comes in III, iii, 438. Othello says simply but with passionate force, 'I'll tear her all to pieces.' The line comes after an excruciating scene in which

Othello is more and more ensnared by Iago. The scene is a slow meticulous process in which Iago entraps Othello in a powerful net of patriarchal ideological forms. They are entirely ideologies of the 'other' to the Moor; he is forced to learn the nature of Venetian social practice by which exclusion and 'othering' cement the central structure. Iago's argument depends upon a notion of female chastity as the basis of patriarchy; upon a society where female power which is rigidly circumscribed by law and custom is possible as deception. Desdemona is constructed as part of that underworld of fearful subversive wives:

> In Venice they do let God see the pranks
> They dare not show their husbands: their best
>   conscience
> Is not to leave undone, but keep unknown.
>
> (III,iii,206−8)

The word 'pranks' has a nice salacious ring, and suggests female sexuality as a natural urge to be promiscuous. Wives are represented here as a conspiratorial unity, ranged in a 'natural' alliance against husbands. How does a Moor in Venice react to such a proposition? We are not told anywhere in the play about Moorish women and their marital arrangements, but the casual suggestion that any Venetian man knows this 'truth' tends to describe the way in which Othello's own outsideness to Venice is the means to his vulnerability. It places him in a special relationship to this body of females, themselves outside the sphere of political power as he himself is. He is not a Venetian husband, and his Venetian wife in behaving just like a Venetian wife extends the distance between himself and the world he has attempted to enter; that same world keeps thwarting that entry through its most plausible interpreter, Iago. Othello's blackness, the sign, as Stephen Greenblatt notes, of all that the society finds frightening and dangerous, 'is the indelible witness to Othello's permanent status as an outsider'.[6]

The trouble is that Desdemona herself makes it easier for Iago; she smoothes his path by acting the woman's part. Desdemona's pleas in Cassio's behalf are not simply acts of friendship, nor can they be. The hierarchical structure of sexual relationships determines that between men and women any relationship has a sexual basis. Desdemona's appeal, that is, cannot be or seem innocent, a fact that Iago grasps more swiftly than Othello, and one he uses with potent effect. The relationship is tinged with sexuality because it was formed within a sexual context of courtship and because, indeed, all relationships have a sexual component. It is a relatively simple matter for Iago to expose what is sexual between Desdemona and Cassio because it is already latent. Iago twice notes the sexuality of the relationship to himself when he comments on Cassio's flirtatious hand-holding with Desdemona (II,i,167–75) and declares his conviction that 'Cassio loves her' (ii,i,281). Within a society which functions through sexual suppression, where one sexual group is determined as inferior to the other, it is entirely reasonable that sexual conflict will arise and manifest itself in the inferior subject group resisting the oppression of the superior. That is to say, female discontentment is created by the very attempt to stifle it. Desdemona from the beginning eagerly fills a masculine ideal of wifeliness as she prepares to subsume herself in her husband's identity; but in doing so reveals her own capacity for resistance which Iago later seizes on. Her words are fraught with this very contradiction:

> That I did love the Moor, to live with him,
> My downright violence, and scorn of fortunes,
> May trumpet to the world: my heart's subdued
> Even to the utmost pleasure of my lord.
>
> (I,iii,248–51)

Her 'downright violence' is her version of the way in which she has willingly broken social convention to win a husband. Subduing her heart to the pleasure of her lord argues a heart that requires taming. In other words the passage implies a powerful *capacity* for resistance in the very lexis by which it declares acquiescence.

Othello is weakened by his own need of that acquiescence. He expresses again and again a profound and urgent desire to be a part of the same society that rejects and uses him. The racial hostility of virtually all of the Venetians, sometimes smooth ('I think this tale would win my daughter too' [I,iii,171] – a far cry from permission to marry) sometimes rough ('her most filthy bargain' [V,ii,158]) seems to intensify his need to prove it wrong. The tentativeness of his relationship with Venice has been much commented on; it is a relationship that his marriage to Desdemona, consciously or not, is designed to address. The black stranger marrying the most eligible virgin in Venice is a fact that is not capable of being innocent however much readers have wanted to believe it to be. Marriage is a political and ideological fact of life and there is nothing innocent or 'natural' about it. The unseen but real *act* of marriage between Othello and Desdemona is a concession to Venice, a hopeful embrace of its codes and ideologies by the self-determined groom and bride, stranger and native inhabitant. There is thus a potent political dimension to the marriage. However, instead of cementing his connection to the society, Othello's marriage succeeds in making that connection more fragile. Venice is now bound to look upon him as more than a stranger-mercenary whom it employs for pay; it must now regard him as a son-in-law, as a potential citizen, as one of them, because he has violently defied their practice by circumventing it through elopement. The marriage thus makes Othello an object of suspicious regard; it is a bold and risky enterprise in that divided world.

By marrying Desdemona and thus declaring himself a bridegroom of the city, Othello cannot toy with Venetian sexual and marital codes, which he may have done previously if Iago's charge that Othello had a sexual relationship with Emilia has substance. His entire identity is caught up with that of Desdemona who represents the Venice of her fathers to him and embodies its customs and laws. In Desdemona Othello has invested his entire and complex identity as a black intruder. The Duke's acceptance of Othello's marriage is not, as some have thought, simply a matter of military convenience to him, but rather an indication of the flexibility of the Venetian polity and the absorptive power of its customs. The aberration present in this marriage will be smoothed out with time. Venetian culture has constructed marriage according to the characteristics of early modern culture described by Greenblatt as a marriage of the active male to the passive female.[7] Othello and Desdemona's marriage, because of the part each plays, and is said to have played in making it happen, is a parody or, perhaps, a travesty, of that norm.

The violent commencement of the union of Othello and Desdemona supplies a crucial part of the logic of Desdemona's murder. It adumbrates in a deliberate way the violence with which this marriage is destined to be accompanied throughout its short life. From the cacophonic overture provided by the raucous villains Iago and Roderigo, the marriage is surrounded more and more closely by the menacing overtones of violent eruption. This comes in the form of monition and prophecy – such as that made by Brabantio

– in the form of a storm, a tavern brawl and, in the hectic language of violent conflict, through the agencies of lexis and metaphor. The countervailing force is the love of the protagonists; against this background they insistently declare their mutual love and faith to the point where the violent world around them begins to penetrate that love. Violence presents itself initially in the form of suspicion – and A. P. Rossiter is right to caution us about the distinction the play makes between suspicion and jealousy[8] – but quickly develops into the kind of dreadful threat of physical suppression that seems so natural to the Iagos and Roderigos of the world. Othello, as has often been noted, absorbs the Iago spirit into his own so that no corner of the world of the play is unpermeated by potential violence against women. He adopts Iago's discourse of rationality. His love of Desdemona, hitherto constructed by him on the basis of the purest romantic feeling, he starts to examine in the narrow rationalist terms of probability: 'And yet how nature erring from itself' (III,iii,231). It is, as we see, a discourse that perpetuates the hierarchical sexual politics of Venice. Iago's misogyny translates itself into a rational system where it is *natural* for women to betray men. In one of the most telling lines of the play, Othello exposes his own misogynistic potential and his own sexual fears:

> O curse of marriage,
> That we can call these delicate creatures ours
> And not their appetites!
>
> (III,iii,272–4)

The lines lament the ultimate inability of the man to possess the woman completely – and, of course, by implication they simultaneously stress the desirability of commanding even their appetites. As Edward Snow has noted, 'The underlying male fear is thralldom to the demands of an unsatisfiable sexual appetite in woman. It is crucial to realize . . . that the threat appears not when something intrinsically evil emerges in Desdemona's will, but when the conventional boundaries of marriage close in upon it.'[9] Brabantio's prophecy in the senate chamber ('Look to her Moor, have a quick eye to see:/ She has deceived her father , may do thee [I,iii,292–3]) becomes, then, the basis of a rational process by which her – and woman's – natural propensity to deceive is predictable. In her 'infidelity' Desdemona has stolen Othello's passage into Venetian patriarchy. In this fact too, reason plays its part, as Iago manages to convince Othello that he does not really or 'naturally' have a place in Venice.

Othello's killing of Desdemona becomes, then, the rational outcome of a process set in motion by a masculine sexual politics. Much has been written about the ways in which Othello is entrapped or, according to Alessandro Serpieri, seduced by Iago.[10] Iago does not steal Othello's soul, but rather he uses a specifically male reasoning to convince Othello of his wife's natural and predictable unfaithfulness. Further, this reasoning is so thoroughly embedded in the Venetian culture as to be convincing to a would-be Venetian who has no way of comprehending its flexibility. Indeed, Othello's value to the senate and to Desdemona herself is his own inflexibility – his soldierly firmness of purpose and uncompromising sense of mission. He comprehends, perhaps as no other, that the order of the patriarchy depends upon female chastity, but cannot accept, as others more sophisticatedly do, that this chastity is not a thing he can control. To Othello, the recognition that he cannot control his wife's sexual being is precisely concomitant with his perception of the inherent weakness of the patriarchal culture he wishes to claim. His need of 'ocular proof' is part of a desperate clinging to the world of materiality, of manageable matters, and it attempts to give a tangible form to this overdetermined quasi-abstraction that is chastity.

Total control of another is only possible through violence and murder. Because of the potential and inherent privacy of sexuality the only absolutely definitive means by which one person may control the sexuality of another is by killing them. For sexual life includes not merely private acts of sex including, of course, masturbation, but also sexual thoughts. It is to this fact of the private nature of sexual life that Iago so effectively speaks when he warns Othello of the 'pranks' of Venetian wives.

The knowledge of Desdemona's power to keep an unknown part of herself to herself does violence to Othello's conception of his relation to the female world; it traduces and subverts his sustaining idea of romantic love where the other becomes utterly absorbed in the self. His possessive and absorbing love of Desdemona, powerful and heroic as it is, cannot accommodate autonomous femaleness. His addresses to her declare his notion of her as a female extension of himself, from his statement that he loved her because she pitied the dangers he had passed, to the sheer pride and joy with which he claims her as his 'fair warrior' (II,i,182), his Desdemona. These linguistic habits are indices to the ideological forms through which Othello constructs Desdemona and his love of her. They argue the absolute inseparability of Desdemona from himself. Iago's proposition – expressed repeatedly and in various ways – that she, like all women, has a private existence, violates this quintessential idea. And this is the reason for Iago's success: once the reality of the potential independence of the other has been declared, there is no way to efface it. The idea lodges like a burr in Othello's mind, it worries his thought incessantly. In his unwillingness to admit a private and autonomous identity to Desdemona, Othello shows much in common with Brabantio. Neely has said that in this play 'romantic love is destroyed by male friendship which itself soon disintegrates'.[11] We may perhaps go farther and suggest that romantic love is doomed by its contingent condition of female submission and can only succeed when that submission is assured by having been willingly entered into by the subject.

By killing Desdemona, Othello determines to resolve the impossible difficulty into which suspicion has placed him. The speech he makes over her sleeping form is precisely a wrestling with the ideology of the male right to dominate women. That is the unhappy given of the entire speech. It is an exquisite homage to an ugly political reality. Desdemona is subsumed in Othello's notion of womankind: he not only refuses to name the cause for which he must kill her, he also does not name Desdemona herself in the entire speech. By the potent absence of her name, Desdemona is de-individuated; as 'she' in the speech, she stands for all women. Just as Othello naming his motive as a general cause of mankind – 'else she'll betray more men' – attempts to distance himself from the act. The terrible tension of the speech comes from its counter movements between the publicly political and the subjectively political; between Othello's attempt to recuperate ideological stability through the social practice of sacrifice and his longing for an innocent Desdemona. The speech is part of a carefully practiced, time-honored performance of sacrifice where victim and priest assume conventional roles with Desdemona cooperatively immobile, 'smooth as monumental alabaster' and Othello, interestingly, as 'Justice herself'. Its ultimate purpose is to renew and recover social value, social stability, and social justice as though these ideas were fixed in natural and pure forms and as though this kind of selfless killing were the chief agency by which such recovery can be accomplished. Part of the reason that Othello depersonalizes Desdemona to the extent that he does not use her name in the speech, that he makes her the sacrificial victim for the sake of 'more men', is precisely to constitute her as the embodiment of a social evil that threatens the fabric of patriarchal authority.

The sad fact is that he is almost right. This point has been taken by readers for centuries. Desdemona's death is regarded as a horrifying wrong because all readers and audiences know that she is innocent of infidelity to Othello. This surely is why Bradley saw *Othello* as the 'the most painfully exciting and the most terrible'[12] of all Shakespeare's tragedies. The advent of a rigourous feminist criticism over the last decade has enabled the acceptance of the idea that the structure of male domination which Othello is attempting to recover is itself the cause of his perception of her infidelity. Or, as Louis Montrose has asserted in another context, the Shakespeare text discloses 'that patriarchal norms are compensatory for the vulnerability of men to the powers of women'.[13] That slightly mysterious thing which Othello is attempting to restore is male control with the unacknowledged intention that the entire political structure will once more be compelled to rest upon a male valuation of female chastity. The inevitable consequence of such a restoration is the reproduction of the conditions by which the same tragedy may be endlessly repeated.

The text itself subverts this assumption. For as Othello prepares himself beautifully and ritualistically to sacrifice his wife in the interest of a larger purpose and a great social value, she wakes. As she does so she resumes another identity than that which he has placed upon her while she sleeps. Sleeping, Desdemona assumes Othello's construction of her as a passive, beautiful participant in a pre-enacted ritual; she is one with the sacrificial victims of the ages. When she wakes she shatters the self-constructed male fantasy of Othello as the soldiering priest of mankind. Her waking insists on her female reality and restores Desdemona to the scene as a living vital presence, capable of feelings of fear and horror, willing to beg for her life, insisting on her innocence. The marmoreal, recumbent, sleeping woman of the long speech now insistently demonstrates her humanity and in doing so actively repudiates the construction of herself by which Othello has been enabled to perform the sacrifice. In this way too, she stands as a reproach to the dreadful oversimplification of 'else she'll betray more men'.

Othello's reproaches to Desdemona once she wakes all take their point of departure from a structure of absolutes which together constitute patriarchy in its most highly idealised form. He refers her to her crimes and sins and urges her to reconcile herself to heaven and grace. Desdemona counters these large abstractions with reference to her own fear. She insistently personalizes her own murder as Othello vainly attempts to cling to the artificial representation of the murder as a ritual cleansing. Othello is again seduced by words into another terrible recognition: he accepts Desdemona's terms that make this murder a murder, and releases in volleys of violent abuse a horrible brutality that may be said to have been concealed by the entire structure of sacrifice he has so carefully created. He is forced to confront the fact that the name of the thing is not the thing itself but its name. Lawrence Danson has noted that the confusion between the words murder and sacrifice 'is the final terminological confusion, attesting to the equivocal nature of the 'reality' beyond language, in a play which has moved from verbal ironies to split between rival semantic systems'.[14] Othello has dressed up murder to look like a grand and beautiful part of a deeply felt faith. Desdemona, waking, forces him to see it for what it is:

> O perjur'd woman, thou dost stone thy heart,
> And makest me call what I intend to do
> A murder, which I thought a sacrifice
>
> (V,ii,64–6)

In this tragic recognition the entire justificatory system of patriarchy collapses. The confrontation of Othello and Desdemona becomes charged with a specifically male brutality that no amount of rationalization can efface. The basis of the sexual relationship under patriarchy is exposed as a power relationship where the stronger dominates. In murdering Desdemona in this frantic fashion without the glamourizing accoutrements of ritual and ceremony, Othello subverts the ideological structure of patriarchal marriage and exposes its passionate reality – the killing of a wife out of sexual jealousy. The method of murder is a metaphor for the male fear of female power. Tennenhouse points out: 'Much as it may seem to diverge from a form of mutilation that displays the permeability of the body, this punishment [of smothering her] also points right to the source of the assault upon patriarchy, the woman's political voice.'[15]

The thing he has so carefully and slowly taught himself to do is destroyed. From his first determination to tear her into pieces,

Othello has with huge difficulty placed increasing emotional and intellectual distance between the feeling of that line and the act of sacrificing his wife. She wakes and the distance disappears. Othello's first determination to kill Desdemona receives many echoes as his jealousy grows, and many of his threats take the same violent and furious form. He will 'chop her into messes'; he strikes and violently abuses her. He behaves, as Neely has said, like a darkened version of the comic cuckold,[16] helplessly berating his wife and hopelessly seeking a remedy for an imagined but irremediable act. His violent rage comes from sexual jealousy and feelings of sexual and social inadequacy. For when Othello determines to tear Desdemona to pieces or chop her up, he is not speaking from a sense of disappointed romantic love or a desire to preserve the institution of marriage, but rather from a sense of fury at having been found sexually inadequate.[17] What Othello calls the 'act of shame' (V,ii,213) and 'filthy deeds' (149) are descriptions of the sex act that tend to expose what Snow calls a 'pathological male animus towards sexuality'[18] found everywhere in Othello's language about sexuality. Between his murderous threats and the 'It is the cause' speech, Othello has created a consolatory network of justification composed of politically and ideologically charged myths which refer to the ultimate truth of patriarchy. Othello has managed for a moment to harness the fury that seethes in him and give it a resting place in political mythology. Desdemona's crime against him, exposing and humiliating him, is a crime against the universal order which has been broken by her challenge to the rule of her fathers. The cause may, as M. R. Ridley maintains, be chastity,[19] but it is as well for us to remember that chastity in this and in all other contexts is a highly loaded term that usually manifests itself through the agency of male domination. For chastity tends to refer to the faithfulness of women to men, as it most certainly does in this play.

Othello's sacrifice in behalf of chastity is a clear attempt to act violently in a good cause. This idea of violence for the public good is discussed by Rene Girard in his description of what he calls the sacrificial crisis. Girard offers a useful distinction between two kinds of violence, both of which are promised in the murder scene of this play. He talks of the sacrificial crisis as the disappearance in a society of the 'difference between impure violence and purifying violence. When this difference has been effaced, purification is no longer possible and impure, contagious, reciprocal violence spreads throughout the community.'[20] Othello's cause is a purifying violence, a killing committed so that social values may be restored. Desdemona's infidelity – and by extension any *female* infidelity – threatens social cohesion. In his sacrifice speech Othello attempts to transform Desdemona into a scapegoat; he concentrates into her all female infidelity, all female sexual treachery, and declares that by killing her he will rescue the society from the evil she contains and represents. Othello desires that his killing of Desdemona will express him. He hopes that in this act will be distilled his love of Desdemona's good, his hatred of her evil, his commitment to Venetian social and legal systems, and his commitment to the Christian religious practice to which he has come later in life. Though it is perhaps unwise to speculate, I think it reasonable to imagine Othello's idea of the post-sacrificial events. Likely, having stifled the lovely Desdemona and not spoiled her features, he would have killed himself in a gesture of equally self-glorifying drama and gone to his death like the brave soldier he is, convinced of the necessity of the action. This expression of himself is possible only if Desdemona will cooperate with his careful, religious, staging of the sacrifice by remaining asleep in her alabaster, immobile state, like the compliant scapegoat of mythology. But she wakes. And in that simple, single act she transforms his sacrifice into a murder.

It is a murder from which the play does not shrink. Indeed, the text seems to revel in the sheer brutality of the killing of Desdemona, giving detailed attention to the abuse, the mental and physical suffering, and the rough, violent conclusion. Othello's rage boils up once again and he stifles Desdemona in a fit of abuse. The terrible words 'Down, strumpet!' (80) accompany Desdemona's murder. That murder is a dreadful inversion of the mellifluous sacrifice he had planned. The drama of the murder is a drama of spontaneity, a killing unaccompanied by the redeeming social value the killer had placed upon the vaunted sacrifice. The murder itself is a mocking echo of that sacrifice, exposing its fraudulence as a purifying agent of the society for which it is performed. The murder as a murder challenges the assumptions upon which the ideology of sacrifice rests. It validates femaleness and female autonomy, the very concepts which the sacrifice was designed to contain and enclose. The man performing the sacrifice in *Othello* is a man determined to put an end to the dangerous and subversive idea of female self-determination. Othello's interest in performing the sacrifice is blatantly identified with that of his fellow *men*. The murder, on the other hand, breaks down the structure of reason and justification; it becomes suddenly, loosely, and brutally, an act of male self-determination and self-interest. In being so transformed, the murder exposes the fragility and the thinness of the veil of self delusion that constitutes the patriarchy of this world.

9

Conclusion: *Macbeth*

The violent act, as we have seen, has been naturalized by patriarchal social formations. Violence stands as one of the most flexible practices in the social structure and has been appropriated in most societies as the prerogative of the state. As a matter of social necessity the unsanctioned use of violence is constructed and understood as contrary to the public interest and is made illegal in order to protect both the potential victims of violence and the interests of those for whom it is a means of control, in particular those who dominate and direct state authority. We need to be careful, of course, to recognize what is meant by the 'state', and to distinguish that entity from the more merely artificial entities which it includes, such as political parties and interest groups whose variety and boldness will depend upon the state's capacity to absorb and contain dissent and opposition. The state is all of its parts as well as the political ideology which determines its modes of maintaining power – only a revolution which replaces that ideology can fundamentally change the form of the state.

In the history plays we are given a partial and limited idea of a state whose flexibility is very restricted. Monarchical power is represented, not always uncritically or favourably in the plays, as tremendously contingent upon conformity. The *Henry* plays discussed in this book, rattle and shake with discontent and internalised opposition. Rebellion and revolution are constantly potential; revolution is upheaval, rebellion a (usually violent) change of personnel and style which continues the old ways. The discontented, rebellious rich are less threatening to the state than the discontented, rebellious poor – as I attempt to show in Chapter 4. The disaffected rich are represented as a capable alternative to the present rule. The poor, on the other hand, are represented as a positive danger to all forms of law and order, stability and social survival: rich rebels may change the succession, but the poor will change the entire state itself beyond recognition; they will bring chaos. Chaos means, in the terms in

126

which it is discussed and implied, the end of difference – gender and hierarchical difference in particular. As the political plays are constructions in different ways of the contingent hierarchical differences of monarchy, so the tragedies I have examined demonstrate the way in which gender has been formed – or deformed – to meet the need of the hierarchical/patriarchal structure to sustain and perpetuate itself. The subjectness of women to men, and the unaltering need to enforce it, is a condition of structural survival. The relation between survival and enforcement is a concern of the plays and, in a general way, the subject of this study.

What is dangerous about *Macbeth* is its amazingly audacious reach into the depths and origins of social categories and its astonishing representations of the ideological basis of categorical difference. The play seems to explore the possibilities of unleashed violence in a world already inured to violence. So that what is normally a violent place has then to absorb ever increasing eruptions of violence to a degree almost beyond measure. This rain of violence in all forms upon an already staggering world only produces corollaries such as the breakdown of 'normal' forms. Gender distinctions, which *Titus, Othello,* and *Lear* have shown to be in perpetual crisis and in perpetual need of restatement and recovery by the dominant ideology, are close to being erased in *Macbeth.* The power of violence is nearly sufficient to perform such erasure. And the recovery of difference at the end of the play is feeble in comparison to the threat that it claims to have contained. Most alarming of all, however, *Macbeth* suggests the terrible seductive power of violence. Indeed that is the context of its beginning. That haunting and terrible beauty that violence can be is pursued to its dreadful but rational conclusions.

Not even Duncan is above taking delight in horrible bloody slaughter. On being told that Macbeth unseamed Macdonwald from the nave to the chops and fixed his head upon the battlements, he cannot suppress a happy exclamation: 'O valiant cousin! worthy gentleman!' (I,ii,24). He is implicated in the violence of the play in the sense that these words suggest; he is attracted to and made part of it, and in death he becomes its central image, from voyeur of violence to its most crucial and evidentiary martyr. Duncan's vicarious pleasure at the violence wrought by Macbeth is inverted as the violence of *Macbeth* is terribly turned against him. Yet his complicity, Jonathan Goldberg argues, is substantial and perceptible in the mirroring effect of the play's three monarchies.[1]

The violence of *Macbeth* is of a different kind than that of the other tragedies. Where it is possible in those plays and in the histories to recognize the potent ritualistic function of violence, to see in the acts of murder the intention to secure social stability by killing, in *Macbeth* undisguised physical violence becomes the only available means of subjugating the social body. Macbeth's initial purpose of entrenching his rule by the sword gives way to the more awesome purpose of killing because killing is easy. The social functions of violence become lost in this play. It is an irony, though a dreadful and ominous one, that the restoration of social stability is signalized holding the butcher's head aloft like Macdonwald's earlier. These actions Howard Felperin regards as totemic deterrents to tyrrany, 'a public symbol of the inviolability of the social order and a glaring reminder of the moral law that sustains it'.[2] It needs to be recognized, however, that this reasonable interpretation of these powerful symbolic acts – which in this light would have pleased King James – overlooks the play's subtle subversion of precisely this view which Duncan's ambiguous role supplies.

Between the two displays of severed heads the perilousness of the rule of violence is inscribed into the drama by the erasure of the normal distinction between positive and negative violence. This erasure is the most dangerous and destructive event imaginable in the life of the social organism and prompts the 'sacrificial crisis'.[3] The ability to distinguish between kinds of violence is the very thing that makes social cohesion possible. That distinction removed, whatever is social breaks down and the community loses its cohesive power as sacrifice itself, in the most primitive and most industrialized societies, loses its function. When the difference between impure violence and purifying violence has been effaced, writes Girard, 'purification is no longer possible and impure, contagious, reciprocal violence spreads throughout the community'.[4] I am arguing that this, in part, is what happens in *Macbeth*; that the distinction between kinds of violence is lost and the resultant carnage is both a logical product of, and itself produces, multiplying breakdowns of related distinctions and differences which sustain the social formation. Macbeth, then, takes us to the very brink of chaos. I am suggesting also that in questioning the received notion of Duncan as a wholly unimplicated victim of Macbeth's ruthless drive for power we can more fully comprehend the extent of this vision of the play. *Macbeth* commences on a note of violence in process, and it sustains that process through the agency of one who is simply the most ruthless exponent of the individualism that drives through the ruling factions. In a curious but seriously political sense, Macbeth is a victim of a world he has been taught to serve in but one in which he has not been taught to stand and wait in. Impatience, after all, is part of what destroys him.

The impulses of the play towards the 'limitlessness' that Stephen Booth proposes as the ubiquitous and dominant effect of this tragedy[5] is also to be seen in the way in which the play constructs the fact and the presence of violence. This play gives a terrible image of limitless violence, violence that has no perceptible origin in the play and no palpable end. As the action begins physical brutality is already well in progress and we see reestablished at the conclusion a monarchy much like the one that produced Macbeth; it is validated, as we have seen, by the impaled head of the king being brutally used as (ambiguous? hypocritical?) evidence that tyranny is dead. The relation of this violence to the polity is profound. Indeed, the tangible reality of Macbeth's evil actions is simultaneously an image of the potential evil of the monarchical system he inherits by bloodshed. Kiernan Ryan makes a similar point when he writes that the tragedy of *Macbeth* is the tragedy of a man driven to become 'quite specifically – a ruthless individualist whose defiant creed is: 'For mine own good / All causes shall give way' (III,iv,134–5). The play pursues 'an unflinching demonstration of the cost of that creed with whose less eloquent, latter-day equivalents . . . we are only too well acquainted'.[6] The kind of individualism that is praised, rewarded, and promoted in Macbeth is based upon achievement that can only be recognized relatively and competitively. Its evidence is not merely the success of an enterprise but, more specifically, the failure of another. Victory can only be ensured by defeat.

The means of promoting the pursuit of success without endangering the social formation is encoded within the politics of patriarchy which protects itself from itself by the valorization of a complex moral system. It is Macbeth's constant awareness of that system in conflict with his most passionate desire to control it that constitutes the tragedy's deepest tension. What moves him, after all, to reconsider killing the king but the most palpable of patriarchal codes?

> First, as I am his kinsman and his subject,
> Strong both against the deed; then as his host,
> Who should against his murtherer shut the door,
>
>   (I,vii,13–15)

There is a banality about these lines; their logic is the logic of the obvious. In this speech it is only when Macbeth recalls Duncan's virtues, his meekness and clearness, that he is moved to really eloquent argument against the murder. It is significant that he does not say here that murder is bad in and of itself; rather he argues that the murder of Duncan would be bad. Part of the reason for this is that murder is an embedded fact of the play from its beginning. Macbeth's killing of Macdonwald is as exciting and horrible in the telling as any other act of violence in the play:

> For brave Macbeth (well he deserves that name),
> Disdaining Fortune, with his brandish'd steel,
> Which smok'd with bloody execution,
> Like Valour's minion, carv'd out his passage,
> Till he fac'd the slave;
> Which ne'er shook hands, nor bade farewell to him,
> Till he unseam'd him from the nave to th'chops,
> And fix'd his head upon our battlements.
>
> (I,ii,16–20)

Violence can have positive value. Here Macbeth is a Jehovah performing righteous murder. The 'unseam'd' adds a grotesquely comic quality[7] to the picture of Macbeth hacking his way through a forest of enemy soldiers and sabotages the dread solemnity of the passage in its idealization of physical prowess. But the narrative casts forth an image of Macbeth as an almost superhuman engine of destruction. The phrase 'carv'd out his passage' is no neutral description of the warrior's progress, but a terrible image of bloody slaughter as Macbeth makes a corridor of bodies between himself and Macdonwald. The smoking sword speaks not only of the hidden demonism of the hero, but also the wrath with which he wreaks his righteous havoc.

All the more revealing then is Duncan's response. This *is* a martial, cruel, brutal world where the act of disloyalty can bring the actor to his death. Treachery is immediately linked to violence and death. But it has become an ubiquitous presence with the first scene where the witches warn of the inversions in the air. Thus, when Macbeth is given the treacherous Thane of Cawdor's title we need to keep hold of the element of coincidence of the bestowal, to remain alert, in other words, to the potential randomness that develops into a proleptic associative act. To acknowledge the acquisition of the title only as a sign is to be trapped into the all too tempting notion of a connected world of transcendental experience where things are self-contained, self-reflexive, and, more seriously, unconnected to history or ourselves. Accidentalism, chance, random and chaotic experience are vital forms of expression and experience in this world. The contrary idea of destiny is an idea of safety – though often paradoxically so – which wrests from us the possibility and responsibility of self-determination. If we take Macbeth's treachery to his king as an act that is predetermined in some way by his having donned the robes of a traitor, we run the risk of surround-ing his tragedy with marks and signs supernaturally laid out for him: of arguing that he is beyond self or social rescue. (It is, of course, possible to read the play within an historical context which stresses, as it must, the influences of Calvinism and providentialism on seventeenth-century England. A political reading, however, is bound to regard these influences as themselves political and subject to a political analysis.)

The way of violence is established by Duncan and Macbeth. And yet, in Duncan's delight at Macbeth's success, is potently repre-sented the difference between righteous and impious violence and rage. While Duncan lives, the difference remains an essential part of a clearly constructed system of differences. Righteous violence and righteous rage are rage and violence directed centrifugally – from the king and his adherents. His monarchy is contingent on this difference being known and adhered to. Macdonwald, precisely, has attempted to reverse the direction of that violence, to erase the difference. His failure constitutes Duncan's success above all; it reaffirms and recovers the line of command, and it reestablishes the 'socially responsible' way for violence to be used. Macbeth is the iron fist of the monarchy turned against its enemies. He knows well and from vivid experience that the supreme proof of established power is its physical superiority. As Goldberg says, '*Macbeth* opens with reports of Macbeth fixing a rebel head upon the battlements and closes with his severed head displayed by Macduff; a plot inscribed and generated within specularity: in each instance, a supposedly saintly king has let another do his dirty work.'[8]

It is this palpably historic and traditional loyalty to patriarchy and its ideology that is the source of the violence of the play – as is even the violence against the arch-patriarch, Duncan. Norman Rabkin claims to have isolated the 'key' to Macbeth's motivation to murder. He finds it in Lady Macbeth's 'mysterious explanation for her own surprising sudden inability to kill Duncan: 'Had he not resembled / My father as he slept, I had done't,' followed immediately by Macbeth's "I have done the deed."'9 She recognizes, Rabkin continues, that the killing of a king is a form of parricide. 'And that is what Macbeth knows, and what impels him to do his deed.'10 The impulsion is also explicable as dread – what Kierkegaard called 'the alarming possibility of *being able*'11 coupled with the knowledge of the prohibition which hedges the act. Macbeth's act of violence against the father breaches one of patriarchy's most powerful and self-protective codes, but it simultaneously enacts the overwhelming primal desire which these codes attempt to suppress. Violence against the father – and, by extension, the constructed father, the king – is represented in this reading of the play as a logical reaction to the inevitable tyranny of the father. It is necessary to stress, as Rabkin does not, that parricide is a *political* act, the internalization of whose impulses is another of the self-protective *means* of the patriarchal politics which has produced and is encoded in the play. King Duncan is generous to Macbeth as Macbeth the warrior is generous to Duncan. But, surely, the fact of Duncan the king is what oppresses Macbeth. It is not ambition for the crown that prompts the thane to the murder of his king, it is that Duncan is king and can be murdered.12

Lady Macbeth's dilemma is less difficult and complex. It is to do the deed without being seen:

> Come, thick Night,
> And pall thee in the dunnest smoke of Hell,
> That my keen knife see not the wound it makes,
> Nor Heaven peep through the blanket of the dark
> (I,v,50–3)

She is, as Jan Kott has said, without imagination; 'and for that reason she accepts herself from the outset, and later cannot escape from herself'.13 To her, as to Duncan, Macbeth is an instrument of conquest and power. She gives Macbeth instruction – as Duncan's very regality gives Macbeth instruction – about how to do a business that will benefit them both. She too sees in Macbeth the means to advance themselves: 'look like th'innocent flower, / But be the serpent under't' (64–5). *look* and *be* suggest seeming and being at clear and deliberate odds. It might, perhaps, be suggested that the bloody and terrible Macbeth whom Duncan is made to imagine in the beginning is no less divided; were that Macbeth not ultimately separable from what Duncan claims to believe is the 'real' Macbeth (Valour's minion) he would have found reason to fear him earlier.

The equation of manliness with violence, a truism in the criticism of *Macbeth*, has a curious double edge. It is from Lady Macbeth that Macbeth himself takes his images of manliness. His fears and scruples, his anxious dependence on his wife's opinions bespeak a sensitive 'femaleness' in his own nature which is visibly belied by her brutality. We are left in a gender limbo:

> Bring forth men-children only!
> For thy undaunted mettle should compose
> Nothing but males. Will it not be receiv'd,
> When we have mark'd with blood those sleepy two
> Of his own chamber, and us'd their very daggers,
> That they have done't?
>
> (I,ii,73–8)

Violence and the thoughts of violence so terrify and excite their practitioners as to blur gender boundaries. Cultural and political acts can lose their moorings in conditions like these. Lady Macbeth's response is instructive:

> Who dares receive it other,
> As we shall make our griefs and clamour roar
> Upon his death?
>
> (77–80)

The word 'roar' brings down the gender barrier between man and wife. It comes from the woman and unites her to the man in a mutual animal noise. Violence in this play is passionate and dehumanizing: its users are plunged into another world of action than the human. They seem to be forced into obedience to different and fearsome imperatives which transform them and dislodge them from the political codes to which they are tied. This, of course, is why violence is called good only when it is directed outward from the social unit and evil when it is turned inward. For it enables men and women to break, cross, ignore, or overcome the strict social limitations of patriarchal laws and understandings. Its danger is just that. The drama is powerfully about such crossings and Lady

Macbeth's anticipations cause her to break her contract with her sex and the patriarchal politics that defines it.

In the murder of Duncan the contradictions of patriarchal political practice are exposed. In the play's greatest representation of violence, difference collapses and categories merge in a terrible chaos of act, thought, and emotion. Lady Macbeth and Macbeth lose distinction as they perform this most heinous of the play's murders; and the patriarchal structure itself becomes here an irresistible incentive to the violence it needs to fear. The merging of the man and the woman in a common purpose of killing transforms them into a curiously desexualized instrument of death; it is as though the violence they commit overwhelms their gender and renders it irrelevant. They kill the king, they kill his grooms. Killing under these conditions of confused identity becomes easy – thought is difficult. Macbeth moving stealthily towards Duncan's chamber about the bloody business, emboldened by the forced imagination of a dagger, waiting for his wife to give the summons to the dreadful deed, is potently connected to her. Macbeth, waiting for his wife to sound the bell, reveals a dependency between them that forecloses the independence which was his glory before the terrible night; his maniacal speech hinges upon the knell that produces the decisive words: 'I go, and it is done: the bell invites me. / Hear it not Duncan; for it is a knell / That summons thee to Heaven, or to Hell' (II,i,62–4). Lady Macbeth emerges inflamed by drink; her comment that 'Had he not resembled / My father as he slept, I had done't' (II,ii,12–13) is rueful, her expectation is excited. An inevitable interdependency has been achieved among the murderers and the victim, and with it a breakdown of the distinction that separates them.

Dennis Biggins makes the related point that in *Macbeth* martial violence and savage bloodshed are linked with sexuality and love, that 'the murder of Duncan is pictured as a deed of quasi-sexual violence'.[14] He describes the ways in which the actions of the witches are barely covert acts of sexual violation of *men*. In Shakespeare, sexual violation on the mortal or human level, on the other hand, is always the violation of women by men in fact and in image. Though he does not explore this difference, Biggins leads us into very complex and self-contradictory territory by illuminating the distinction between kinds of sexual violation in *Macbeth*.[15] He argues that the murder of Duncan is constructed by a masculinized Lady Macbeth and her husband as a highly eroticized act. 'Murder is like an unnatural, or nonhuman, sexual act' to Lady Macbeth, who explicitly parallels sexual action with murderous action, while to her husband it is an act of ravishment.[16] Violence, then, as committed by witches and mortals alike, tends to distort the sexuality of its perpetrators. It plunges them into realms of the demonic where the sexual violation of a man can be committed only by a preternatural being like a bearded witch. Its lure transforms women into female men like Lady Macbeth who can describe her grim relish at the thought of dashing out the brains of her own child. It can transform the murderer himself into a ravishing Tarquin. The patriarchal forms, even of violence, have been robbed of their authority by the limitless capacity of violence for transformations that cross forbidden and so-called natural boundaries.

It is perhaps Stephen Booth's notion of the limitlessness of the energies of the play that best describes the mad chaos that murder has become in *Macbeth* as it has not in the other tragedies. Above all else, patriarchy is a system of strictly maintained differences: it is dependent upon those differences – sexual and class differences in particular – being acknowledged by all members of the social formation. Murder in the other tragedies is often represented as an ultimate effort to re-establish those differences when they have been threatened. Among the terrors held by the limitlessness of *Macbeth* is that of the potential displacements of the differences of gender and class. This potential is adumbrated by the witches in the play's very first scene and hedges every example of difference within the drama. The confusion of gender is of a piece with the other confusions of difference and is only its most extreme example. Macduff's cry that 'Confusion now hath made his masterpiece!' (II,iii,67) suddenly constructs the bloody corpse of the king as the site whereupon distinction has been lost, differences fused. The ambiguity of 'Confusion' and the oxymoron of Confusion's masterpiece spin off such possibilities in conformity with the infi-nite meanings produced by the complementary and contradictory images and actions of the drama. Macbeth's agonized description of the corpse produces a vast complex of ambiguities and ironies:

> Who can be wise, amaz'd, temperate and furious,
> Loyal and neutral, in a moment? No man:
> Th'expedition of my violent love
> Outrun the pauser, reason. – Here lay Duncan;
> His silver skin lac'd with his golden blood;

And his gash'd stabs look'd like a breach in nature
For ruin's wasteful entrance: there, the murtherers,
Steep'd in the colours of their trade, their daggers
Unmannerly breech'd with gore. Who could refrain,
That had a heart to love, and in that heart
Courage, to make's love known?

(II,iii,108–18)

This passionate speech explicitly concentrates upon the plethora of contradictions inscribed onto the corpse. Each contradiction, strengthened, not marred, by the lunatic hypocrisy of the speaker issues from the erupting oppositions exposed by the anticipation and excitement which result from the breakdown of order-sustaining differences that have led up to this moment. In this dreadful speech, Macbeth is making a desperate bid to recuperate and reaffirm the value of the categories which have been slowly but surely crumbling since the first words of the play. Macbeth has been an enabler *and* a victim of the malevolent impulse of the driving individualism that has led him to this moment. In seeking to push the ideology of this world to its logical limit, in seeking to use his best skill of violence in its pursuit, he has almost incidentally destroyed himself. Small wonder then that he should be bursting with the passion that sees that destruction and would hold it at bay. Macbeth's and Lady Macbeth's use of violence has unavoidably exceeded its own limit. The series of antitheses at the beginning of the speech are concentrated descriptions of the Macbeth that Macbeth would be. The answer to his own question – 'No man' – constitutes a recognition of the failure of his ambition to absorb all contradictions into himself. Even the dead body of Duncan is a beautiful and terrible emblem of the yoked opposites of silver and gold – 'His silver skin lac'd with his golden blood' – that also ironically and traditionally complement each other.

Macbeth's questions at this grim moment are implicit assertions of the persistent stability of the differences that he has sought to overcome. Wisdom and amazement, temperateness and fury, loyalty and neutrality are constructed antitheses embedded in the patriarchal code of distinction, and it is to them and it that he refers in this panic of dissolution, almost, it seems, as a way of recalling Duncan from the dead. The colliding oppositions take us backwards as surely as they take us forward. They compel recollection of the deeply felt farewell to renown and grace – 'from this instant, /

There's nothing serious in mortality; / All is but toys' (92–4) – as surely as they propel the action onward to an increasingly fragmenting future. The world is breaking up with the death of Duncan, princes flee and distinction and order start collapsing, held together only by the most fragile and unreliable of ties, a king of despair.

However much he has attempted to free himself from the constraints of the old order by destroying its centre, Macbeth's reaction to the death of Duncan reveals the extent to which he is tied to that old order. His representation of Duncan as a holily ordained monarch – silver skin laced with golden blood flamboyantly gives form to the idea of monarchical difference – produces the attempt to replace that monarch with himself. By establishing himself as king, Macbeth demonstrates his need to restore the difference that he has caused to be blurred. But events have outrun his desire; violence has its own laws:

> *Rosse.* And Duncan's horses (a thing most strange and
>   certain)
> Beauteous and swift, the minions of their race,
> Turn'd wild in nature, broke their stalls, flung out,
> Contending 'gainst obedience, as they would make
> War with mankind.
> *Old Man.* 'Tis said, they eat each other.
>
> (II,iv,14–19)

Like many such scenes in the tragedies, this one has the effect of declaring the relatedness of events, the dreadful centrality of human affairs in a contingent universe. If Duncan's horses are eating one another, it is because, simply, Macbeth has killed the king. But the use of nature here, as exemplifying the breakdown of order signifies in another way as well. The loss of distinction signified by the image of carnivorous and cannibalistic horses is also a loss of the distinction of the species protecting itself, a loss, in other words, of 'natural' self protection. As in the human world the indiscriminate practice of violence has led to the loss of distinction between kinds of violence, so the breakdown of difference in the animal world intensifies in the magnificent image the same sense of loss.

In the inexorable disintegration of the social and stable elements of the *Macbeth* world is a compelling representation not of the validity of patriarchy but, more sinisterly, a representation of its invincibly entrenched power. Deep within the complexly inter-woven strands of this form of social order are the ramifying and interdependent means of sustaining and controlling the body politic. To kill the king, as the history plays have shown, is not the same thing as destroying the monarchy itself. Killing the king brings forth only another king. *Macbeth* is merely the most radical of such demonstrations. In the histories violence is a means of replacing the present monarch with another monarch. In *Macbeth* violence is used to explode the very monarchy itself and to shake the foundations of patriarchy and its associated codes of difference and entrenched power structures. In *Macbeth* violence very nearly succeeds in erasing difference; in the histories, on the other hand, violence is used to reaffirm difference.

The greatness of *Macbeth* is, in part, its sheer capacity to confront danger. It is obvious that its hero confronts danger as a daily diet, but the play goes further by dragging the political bases of its culture to the brink of an ideological extinction – a point of despair so terrible and encompassing as to make the mere brutality of patriarchy seem benign. This process is most vivid and notable in the way the drama lays bare the vulnerability of patriarchy by demonstrating that the potent and stable patriarchal forms are not impregnable. The breaking up of patriarchy is very nearly accomplished by the release of a reckless, undifferentiating violence.

Part of the horror of the witches is their almost playful defiance of difference. Critics have been unanimous in their reading of the witches as grim and nightmarish figures. They permeate the world of the play releasing a kind of poison into its very air. The witches' comic wit and vicious joking only exacerbate this quality of monstrosity that they supply. The mischief they wreak is largely a function of their almost violent conflation of abstractions and tangibles. Their predictions are fascinating and ghastly because they blend incompatible elements. The practice commences in the first scene with a variety of such conflations; they dwell in the intangible world of the oxymoron 'When the battle's lost and won' (I,i,4) supplies mystery, paradox, peculiarity. But 'the fog and filthy air' (12) lends a new dimension to paradox. If air is a traditionally pure and spiritual element, what makes it filthy? Fog is not the same as air; the fog is not described as filthy. The words bring into a new and demonic relationship the normally separate elements. That is, they confuse the entire and quintessential structure of difference. If air has become filthy then other differences are less certain than they have been.

A. P. Rossiter notes the suggestion of devastation of difference which the witches supply. He writes that all 'destructive and disordered phenomena are associated with them; and most often those phenomena that devastate human society . . . A similar, but subtly different, quality of suggestion is in the ingredients of the cauldron: poison; parts of repulsive, dangerous, cold-blooded, night-flying beasts; the sweat of a murderer's gibbet; the strangled bastard's finger: everything is obscene, grotesque and out-of-place in a nature men normally associate with kindliness, peace and bounty.'[17] It is this very threat of the fragmentation of patriarchy that patriarchy depends upon and employs as one of the compelling arguments in its favour. The witches, with their potential and actual capacity to break natural and unnatural bounds are therefore the most threatening political force of the drama of *Macbeth*. For they possess a partial control over nature and can thus compel us to see the terrors of a world whose difference has collapsed. It is Macbeth's willing and active penetration of that world that makes him fearsome.

Furthermore, if Dennis Biggins is correct in claiming that the witches's speeches are full of sexual threats to men; in other words if these non-human, man–woman creatures are sexually frightening succubi, then their threat to the patriarchal notions of natural difference are grave indeed, especially if they menace men with sexual violence, as in these and many other lines cited by Biggins:[18]

> And like a rat without a tail;
> I'll do, I'll do, and I'll do.
>
> (I,iii,9–10)

It is indeed the witches and the witch-world of the play that appropriates sexuality. Lady Macbeth's desire to be unsexed only advances and contributes to the burgeoning deformation of sexual and gender differences which are determined by the witches. Their active fragmentation of dividing boundaries of good and bad violence, of man and woman, is central to the energies of violence and violation in the drama.

It is hard to estimate the amount of disturbance that the witches cause in the tragedy. This is not so only because they are malevolent;

rather it has to do with their capacity to subvert and surmount everything mortal. There from the beginning, they appear to generate the action. They linger in the memories of Macbeth and the reader as all-capable force, sheer power, hugely above and beyond the power of ordinary humanity. With the evidence of such preterhuman capability, it is a work of enormous courage to expend ordinary energy, as Macbeth does, in paltering with human limitation and human constructions of value. That good and evil can matter to Macbeth after his encounter with the witches, that he can still desire to maintain and comprehend moral distinction, is a tribute to his courage. For the subversion of difference is the truly radical act. To accomplish or attempt this it is necessary to occupy the position that challenges the patriarchal moral structure. As Lady Macbeth herself constructs an almost gender-free persona for herself, transgressing the boundaries of sexual difference, so Macbeth's criminal violence is a radical subversion of the hierarchical difference which imprisons him. In striking out in this way the play seems more and more to lose its mooring in patriarchy. The spokespeople for patriarchy, including Lady Macduff, are feeble next to Macbeth who plunges with a kind of mad, desperate relish from one calamity to the next.

Macbeth's address to Banquo's murderers is an example of the violent anomaly of his position, of the way in which he is an inherent part of the difference he is engaged in smashing. Patriarchy depends upon difference being sustained. Moral difference is maintained within its limits and, in an ultimate way, by the fixity of the distinction between good and bad violence. The play aspires to transgress difference while the speech reasserts it as a permanent force:

> Ay, in the catalogue ye go for men;
> As hounds, and greyhounds, mongrels, spaniels, curs,
> Shoughs, water-rugs, and demi-wolves, are clept
> All by the names of dogs: the valu'd file
> Distinguishes the swift, the slow, the subtle,
> The housekeeper, the hunter, every one
> According to the gift which bounteous Nature
> Hath in him clos'd; whereby he does receive
> Particular addition, from the bill
> That writes them all alike; and so of men.
> Now, if you have a station in the file,

Not i' the worst rank of manhood, say't;
And I will put that business in your bosoms,
Whose execution takes your enemy off,
Grapples you to the heart and love of us,
Who wear our health but sickly in his life,
Which in his death were perfect.

(III,i,91–107)

The terrible and self-hating speech projects onto the murderers more than just a debased version of human structures; it situates them, and hence the speaker, in a naturalized and remarkably precise order – 'According to the gift which bounteous Nature/ Hath in him clos'd'. In this sense it is a kind of capitulation to the system of difference that the play has called into question and that Macbeth in his maniacally violent fashion has attempted to destroy. The word 'catalogue', placed as it is, is masterly. For it restores the struggle of the play, through the use of a crisply consonantal word, to the blunt world of things: the speech makes this restoration more specific and tangible by the list and variety of species that follow. In a perverse way this speech celebrates the triumph of difference as it simultaneously adumbrates Macbeth's doom in its submission to the categories of Nature and hence the patriarchal structure which has generated this explosive rebellion in the first place.

Patriarchy and its self-sustaining illusional belief systems like Nature and difference are by definition oppressive, even oppressive to the oppressors. Macbeth, a prop and pillar of the ruling class, is dominated by the ideological forms of that very class. The oppression is, of course, relative; it is psychological and metaphysical. Macbeth is not, like the murderers, a mere man who kills for a living. He is a part of the governing fraction and kills out of terrible and tortured desire to defy the systematized power complex that maintains and controls him. Violence is his way of life and violence is the blood and bones of the nation he helps maintain. Macbeth only proves to himself that there is a logic and a morality to the practice of violence. But as he makes this proof he finds too that the logic and morality issue from the patriarchal reality which, simply, proves itself inescapably capacious. The chaotic demolition that the regicide causes submits ultimately to its own oppressive ideology.

Notes

CHAPTER 1: INTRODUCTION

1. Jean Howard describes the ways in which the antitheatrical literature of the period uses the alleged theatricality of women as yet another means of discrediting and diminishing them. 'Renaissance antitheatricality and the politics of gender and rank in *Much Ado About Nothing*', *Shakespeare Reproduced: The text in history and ideology*. Edited by Jean E. Howard and Marion F. O'Connor (London: Methuen, 1987), p. 168.
2. Raymond Williams, *Culture* (Glasgow: Fontana Press, 1981), p. 26.
3. Jonathan Dollimore, *Radical Tragedy: Religion, Ideology, and Power in the Drama of Shakespeare and his Contemporaries* (Chicago: University of Chicago Press, 1984), p. 269.
4. Peter Stallybrass, 'Patriarchal Territories: The Body Enclosed'. *Rewriting the Renaissance: The Discourses of Sexual Difference in Early Modern Europe*. Edited By Margaret W. Ferguson, Maureen Quilligan, and Nancy J. Vickers (Chicago: University of Chicago Press, 1986), p. 133.
5. Leonard Tennenhouse, 'Violence done to women on the Renaissance stage', *The Violence of Representation: Literature and the history of violence*. Edited by Nancy Armstrong and Leonard Tennenhouse (London and New York: Routledge, 1989), p. 80. Louis Montrose, on the other hand, argues for a more disturbed patriarchy under Elizabeth: 'All forms of public and domestic authority in Elizabethan England were vested in men: in fathers, husbands, masters, teachers, preachers, magistrates, lords. It was *inevitable* (my italics) that the rule of a woman who was unmastered by any man would generate peculiar tensions within such a "patriarchal" society.' *A Midsummer Night's Dream* and the Shaping Fantasies of Elizabethan Culture: Gender, Power, Form' *Rewriting the Renaissance*, p. 68.

CHAPTER 2: THE CONTAINMENT OF MONARCHY: *RICHARD II*

1. Leonard Tennenhouse, *Power on Display: The politics of Shakespeare's genres* (Methuen: London and New York, 1986), p. 79.
2. Louis Althusser, *For Marx* (Allen Lane: London, 1969), p. 99.
3. All Shakespeare quotations are from the Arden editions.
4. Moody E. Prior, *The Drama of Power: Studies in Shakespeare's History Plays* (Evanston: Northwestern University Press, 1973) p. 154.
5. Norman Rabkin, *Shakespeare and the Problem of Meaning* (Chicago: University of Chicago Press, 1981) p. 36.

6. Norman Rabkin, *Shakespeare and the Common Understanding* (Chicago: University of Chicago Press, 1867) p. 95.

7. E. M. W. Tillyard, *Shakespeare's History Plays* (Harmondsworth: Penguin, 1962) pp. 245–6.

8. Jonathan Goldberg, *James I and the Politics of Literature: Shakespeare, Spenser, Donne and Their Contemporaries* (Baltimore: The Johns Hopkins University Press, 1983).

9. Harry Berger Jr., 'Psychoanalyzing the Shakespeare text: the first three scenes of the *Henriad*,' *Shakespeare and the Question of Theory*, ed. Patricia Parker and Geoffrey Hartman (New York: Methuen, 1985) p. 215.

10. Robert Ornstein, *A Kingdom for a Stage: the Achievement of Shakespeare's History Plays* (Cambridge: Harvard University Press, 1972) p. 124.

11. Tillyard, p. 250.

12. *Power on Display*. pp. 76–81.

13. Kristian Smidt, *Unconformities in Shakespeare's Histories* (London: Macmillan, 1982) p. 97.

14. Stephanie Jed, 'The scene of tyranny: Violence and the humanistic tradition', *The Violence of Representation*, p. 31.

15. Quoted by John Baxter, *Shakespeare's Poetic Styles: Verse into Drama* (London: Routledge Kegan Paul, 1980) p. 122.

16. Baxter, p. 122.

17. Rabkin, *Shakespeare and the Common Understanding*, p. 90.

18. Prior, p. 141.

19. Joseph Porter, *The Drama of Speech Acts: Shakespeare's Lancastrian Tetralogy* (Berkeley: University of California Press, 1979) p. 21.

20. James L. Calderwood, *Shakespearean Metadrama* (Minneapolis: University of Minnesota Press, 1971) p. 165.

21. Nancy Armstrong and Leonard Tennenhouse, 'Introduction: Representing Violence, or "how the west was won"', *The Violence of Representation*, p. 9.

22. Terry Eagleton, *William Shakespeare* (Oxford: Basil Blackwell, 1986) p. 12.

CHAPTER 3: THE LEGITIMATION OF VIOLENCE IN 1 *HENRY IV*

1. Northrop Frye, *Fools of Time* (Toronto: University of Toronto Press, 1967), p. 4.

2. In *The Scapegoat* (London: Macmillan, 1913), p. 227) James Frazer discusses the role and function of that human being upon whom the evils and sorrows of the society are concentrated and through the death of whom the society is released from its suffering. The process of Hotspur's death suggests that he is Hal's and the nation's scapegoat. Frazer remarks the many ceremonies in primitive and ancient societies whereby regeneration and purification were possible only after the killing of a human scapegoat or the death of a god.

3. In describing dramatic climax, Fredson Bowers emphasizes the

conscious ethical decision of that moment in the drama which determines the inevitability of its outcome. He argues that 'the rising complications of the action culminate in a crucial decision by the protagonist, the nature of which constitutes the turning point of the play and will dictate the . . . catastrophe' ('The Structure of *King Lear*', *Shakespeare Quarterly*, 31 (1980), 7–20; p. 8).

4. Lawrence Danson, *Tragic Alphabet* (New Haven and London: Yale University Press, 1974), pp. 20–1.

5. If the status of Hal as hero is acknowledged, we must recognize that it is owed in large measure to the sheer stage power of the soliloquy. Hal's presumption in addressing us directly – if the 'you' is the audience as much as or more than the departing friends – has the effect of placing him uppermost; he goes beyond the audible reflection of, say, Falstaff on honour, to the point of taking *us* into his confidence, promising *us* a happy surprise and then, here, realizing that promise.

6. Virginia M. Carr, 'Once More into the Henriad: A "Two-Eyed" View', *Journal of English and Germanic Philology*, 77 (1978), 530–45; p. 535.

7. Carr's references to the gradualism of the reintroduction of ceremonies which integrate their primitive substances is consistent with the prince's so-called 'lysis' conversion, described by Sherman Hawkins as one which 'may include more than one crisis experience separated by periods of steady advance' ('The Structural Problem of *Henry IV*', *Shakespeare Quarterly*, 33 (1982), 278–301); p. 296. I am suggesting that Hal's use of ritual in this scene is more significant than a single stage of development or an advance to his next strength: he is demonstrating, by this use of the language of ritual, his own actual control of a situation which by rights belongs to the monarch. King Henry's subjection to this control is signalized by the conviction of his acceptance of the vow.

8. Rene Girard, *Violence and the Sacred* (Baltimore: Johns Hopkins University Press, 1979), p. 37.

9. James L. Calderwood, '*1 Henry IV*: Art's Gilded Lie', *English Literary Renaissance*, 3 (1973), 131–44; p. 137.

10. Maynard Mack, 'The Jacobean Shakespeare', in *Jacobean Theatre*, ed. John Russell Brown and Bernard Harris, Stratford-upon-Avon Studies, I (1960), pp. 11–41; p. 13.

11. Norman Council, 'Prince Hal: Mirror of Success', *Shakespeare Studies*, 7(1974), 125–46; pp. 142–3.

12. Harold Jenkins, *The Structural Problem in Shakespeare's Henry the Fourth* (London: Methuen, 1956), p. 9.

13. George Hibbard, *The Making of Shakespeare's Dramatic Poetry* (Toronto: University of Toronto Press, 1981), p. 180.

14. Herbert Hartmann, 'Prince Hal's "Shewe of Zeale"', *PMLA*, 46 (1931), 720.

15. Girard, p. 37.

16. J. Dover Wilson, *The Fortunes of Falstaff* (Cambridge: Cambridge University Press, 1964), p. 67.

17. *Ibid.* p. 89.
18. J. I. M. Stewart, *Character and Motive in Shakespeare* (Oxford: Oxford University Press, 1965), p. 138.

CHAPTER 4:   THE CULTURE OF VIOLENCE IN *2 HENRY IV*

1. Jonathan Dollimore, '*Introduction*: Shakespeare, cultural materialism and the new historicism,' *Political Shakespeare* (Ithaca and London: Cornell University Press, 1985), p. 5.
2. David Margolies, 'Teaching the handsaw to fly: Shakespeare as a hegemonic instrument,' *The Shakespeare Myth*, ed. Graham Holderness (Manchester: Manchester University Press, 1988), p. 52.
3. Margot Heinemann, 'How Brecht Read Shakespeare', *Political Shakespeare: New Essays in Cultural Materialism*, edited by Jonathan Dollimore and Alan Sinfield (Ithaca: Cornell University Press, 1985), p. 225.
4. Stephen Greenblatt, editor, *The Power of Forms in the English Renaissance* (Norman: Pilgrim Books, 1982), p. 5.
5. J. Dover Wilson, *The Fortunes of Falstaff* (Cambridge: Cambridge University Press, 1964).
6. Brian Vickers, *The Artistry of Shakespeare's Prose* (London: Methuen, 1979), p. 6.
7. Jonathan Dollimore, 'Transgression and surveillance in *Measure for Measure*' *Political Shakespeare*, p. 77.
8. C. L. Barber, *Shakespeare's Festive Comedy* (Princeton: Princeton University Press, 1972), p. 214.
9. Elliot Krieger, *A Marxist Study of Shakespeare's Comedies* (London: Macmillan, 1979), p. 133. I am in less confident agreement with Krieger's notion of Falstaff as an opponent of the images and institutions of authority, having perfect faith in his machiavellian instincts for power, which he employs misguidedly in selecting the subtle prince as his means for acquiring it.
10. Jonathan Goldberg, *James I and the politics of Literature: Jonson, Shakespeare, Donne and Their Contemporaries* (Baltimore, 1983), p. 236.
11. Stephen Greenblatt, 'Invisible bullets: Renaissance authority and its subversion, *Henry IV* and *Henry V*,' *Political Shakepeare*, p. 28.
12. In *Part 1* after the Gad's Hill episode, Falstaff suggests that Hal and Poins are cowards. Hal pretends not to understand the reference, Poins takes a more immediate, spontaneous kind of umbrage, as though in the midst of this joke there are some things that cannot be joked about, and threatens Falstaff with slightly alarming realism: "Zounds, ye fat paunch, and ye call me coward by the Lord I'll stab thee' (II,iv,141–2).
13. This is of course an assertion that accepts the notion that in Shakespeare's plays the prose is produced as being more 'realistic' than verse; that it is more imitative of ordinary English speech than is verse.

14. 'Invisible bullets', p. 41.
15. *The Fortunes of Falstaff*, p. 118.

CHAPTER 5: MONOPOLIZING VIOLENCE: *HENRY V*

1. Mary Douglas, *Natural Symbols* (London, 1973), p. 89. quoted by Werner L. Gundersheimer, 'Patronage in the Renaissance: An Exploratory Approach', *Patronage in the Renaissance*, edited by Guy Fitch Lytle and Stephen Orgel (Princeton, New Jersey: Princeton University Press, 1981), p. 13.
2. Ralph Berry, *The Shakespearean Metaphor* (London: Macmillan, 1978), p. 49.
3. Anne Barton, 'The King Disguised: The Two Bodies of Henry V.' Harold Bloom, editor, *William Shakespeare's Henry V* (New York: Chelsea House Publishers, 1988), p. 18.
4. Coppelia Kahn, '"Magic of bounty": *Timon of Athens*, Jacobean Patronage, and Maternal Power', *Shakespeare Quarterly* 39 (1987), p. 43.
5. Norman Rabkin, *Shakespeare and the Problem of Meaning*, p. 51.
6. James R. Siemon, 'The "Image Bound": Icon and Iconoclasm in *Henry V*', Bloom ed., p. 83.
7. Barton, p. 16.
8. Jonathan Dollimore and Alan Sinfield, 'History and Ideology: The Instance of *Henry V*.' *Alternative Shakespeares*, ed. John Drakakis (London: Methuen, 1985), p. 216.
9. *King Henry V*, ed. John Dover Wilson (Cambridge: Cambridge University Press, 1864), p. xliii.
10. Berry, *The Shakespearean Metaphor* p. 55.
11. Berry, p. 49.

CHAPTER 6: KILLING WOMEN: *TITUS ANDRONICUS*

1. Ian Donaldson, *The Rapes of Lucretia* (Oxford: Clarendon Press), p. 19.
2. Donaldson, p. 23.
3. Lawrence Danson, *Tragic Alphabet: Shakespeare's Drama of Language* (London: Yale University Press, 1974), p. 12.
4. Stallybrass, p. 127.
5. It is true that occasionally in drama of a slightly later period the woman was married off to the rapist thereby helping to supply a pseudo-comic ending to the play. See Suzanne Gossett, '"Best Men are Molded out of Faults": Marrying the Rapist in Jacobean Drama', *ELH* 14 (August, 1984) 3, pp. 305–27.
6. Madelon Gohlke, '"I wooed thee with my sword": Shakespeare's Tragic Paradigms', *Representing Shakespeare: New Psychoanalytic Essays*, edited by Murray M. Schwartz and Coppelia Kahn (Baltimore: The Johns Hopkins University Press, 1980), p. 180.

7. Those plays are *Titus, The Revenger's Tragedy,* Heywood's *The Rape of Lucrece,* and Fletcher's *Valentinian.* Suzanne Gossett provides a thorough general discussion of the dramatic representations of rape in the period 1594 to 1624. See '"Best Men are Molded out of Faults": Marrying the Rapist'.

8. Tennenhouse, 'Violence done to women on the Renaissance stage,' *The Violence of Representation,* p. 83.

9. This year in Stratford, Ontario, the play is performed as a bloody farce. This, surely, is to overcome the absurdity of the accumulated horrors of the text.

10. Douglas E. Green, 'Interpreting "her martyr'd signs": Gender and Tragedy in *Titus Andronicus', Shakespeare Quarterly* 40 (Fall, 1989), 321.

11. ibid.

12. Catherine R. Stimpson, 'Shakespeare and the Soil of Rape,' *The Woman's Part: Feminist Criticism of Shakespeare,* ed. Carolyn Ruth Swift Lenz, Gayle Greene, and Carol Thomas Neely (Urbana: University of Illinois Press, 1980), p. 60.

13. See Derek Cohen, 'The Patriarchal Structure of Jealousy in *Othello* and *The Winter's Tale'. Modern Language Quarterly,* September, 1987.

CHAPTER 7: THE KILLING OF CORDELIA

1. For a witty and irascible account of the critical tendency to mystify tragedy beyond the reaches of reason, see Kiernan Ryan, *Shakespeare* (Hemel Hempstead: Harvester Wheatsheaf, 1989), pp. 44–51.

2. This is not to say that they are not meaningful experiences. But rather that to wrest meaning from them is not possible without resorting to the structures implicit in the access to literary meaning through 'identification with' or universality of the represented experience.

3. See Ralph Berry, 'Lear's System', *Shakespeare Quarterly,* 35, No. 4 (Winter, 1984), 21–29. This essay brilliantly explains the rationality of Lear's decision to divide the kingdom.

4. Jonathan Goldberg, 'Shakespearean inscriptions: the voicing of power', *Shakespeare and the Question of Theory* ed. Patricia Parker and Geoffrey Hartman (New York: Methuen, 1985), p. 133.

5. Henry Fuseli's huge, dramatic nineteenth-century depiction of the banishment of Cordelia is enormously dependent upon the disposition of ranks among those present, with the order of king and nobles arranged – in a characteristic triangle – according to their closeness to the top border of the painting. The three women occupy separate but ranked status with Cordelia and Kent closest to the ground. The painting provides a potent vision of the patriarchy at its most majestic. It may be seen in the Art Gallery of Ontario.

6. Lawrence Danson, *Tragic Alphabet: Shakespeare's Drama of Language* (New Haven: Yale University Press, 1974), p. 166. Danson's reading of Cordelia's speech is representative of the large majority of such readings.

7. Jonathan Dollimore, *Radical Tragedy*, p. 196.
8. *Radical Tragedy*, p. 193.
9. Stephen Greenblatt, 'Invisible bullets: Renaissance authority and its subversion, *Henry IV* and *Henry V'*, *Political Shakespeare*, ed. Jonathan Dollimore and Alan Sinfield (Ithaca: Cornell University Press, 1985), p. 41.
10. I would point out that his best known reference to the poor is quite gender-specific. He talks of 'unaccommodated *man'*.
11. Kathleen McLuskie, 'The patriarchal bard: feminist criticism and Shakespeare: *King Lear* and *Measure for Measure'*, *Political Shakespeare*, p. 106.
12. *Radical Tragedy*, p. 191.
13. Coppelia Kahn, 'The Absent Mother in *King Lear'*, *Rewriting the Renaissance*, p. 48.
14. 'The Absent Mother in *King Lear'*, p. 49.
15. *Radical Tragedy*, pp. 189–202.

CHAPTER 8:   THE MURDER OF DESDEMONA

1. Karen Newman, '"And wash the Ethiop white": femininity and the monstrous in *Othello*,' *Shakespeare Reproduced: The text in history and ideology* (New York: Methuen, 1987), p. 144.
2. Newman, p. 153.
3. Carol Thomas Neely, 'Women and men in *Othello'* *The Woman's Part: Feminist Criticism of Shakespeare*, edited by Carolyn Ruth Swift Lenz, Gayle Greene, and Carol Thomas Neely (Urbana: University of Illinois Press, 1980), p. 218.
4. Thomas Rhymer, 'A Short View of Tragedy', Spingarn, J. E. ed. *Critical Essays of the Seventeenth Century* (Bloomington: Indiana University Press, 1957), p. 221.
5. The point has been made that Othello's apology for his life as presented to the Senate insistently defines not his likeness to the Venetians and his consequent fitness as Desdemona's husband, but rather – and defiantly – his difference from them as his chief qualification. Derek Cohen, *Shakespearean Motives* (London: Macmillan, 1988), p. 92.
6. Stephen Greenblatt, *Renaissance Self-Fashioning: From More to Shakespeare* (Chicago: University of Chicago Press, 1980), p. 240.
7. Greenblatt, writes, 'It is, of course, characteristic of early modern culture that male submission to narrative is conceived as active, entailing the fashioning of one's own story . . . and female submission as passive, entailing the entrance into marriage'. *Renaissance Self-Fashioning*, p. 239.
8. A. P. Rossiter, *Angel With Horns* (New York: Theatre Arts Books, 1961), pp. 189–95.
9. Edward A. Snow, 'Sexual Anxiety in the Male Order of Things in *Othello'*, *ELR*, 10 (1980) p. 407.

10. Serpieri talks of Iago's seduction of Othello as accomplished by the use of a litotes which 'insinuates an affirmation by emphasizing it under the guise of a negation, and unreal affirmation which therefore cannot be expressed directly'. 'Reading the signs: towards a semiotics of Shakespearean drama', translated by Keir Elam. *Alternative Shakespeares*, p. 132.

11. Neely, p. 225.

12. A. C. Bradley, *Shakespearean Tragedy* (London: Macmillan, 1962), p. 143.

13. Montrose, 'The Shaping Fantasies of Elizabethan Culture', p. 77.

14. Lawrence Danson, *Tragic Alphabet: Shakespeare's Drama of Language* (New Haven: Yale University Press, 1974), p. 117.

15. Tennenhouse, *Power on Display*, p. 127.

16. Neely, p. 228.

17. Cassio possesses known and demonstrable sex appeal that makes him an appropriate figure in the fantasies of the jealous husband, fantasies made more vivid by the fact that Othello has admired and identified with him. See Derek Cohen, 'Patriarchy and Jealousy in *Othello* and *The Winter's Tale*', *Modern Language Quarterly*, 48, 3 (September, 1987), p. 207–8.

18. Snow, p. 388.

19. *Othello*, edited by M. R. Ridley (London: Methuen, 1965), p. 177.

20. Girard, *Violence and the Sacred*, p. 49.

CHAPTER 9: CONCLUSION: *MACBETH*

1. Jonathan Goldberg, 'Speculations: *Macbeth* and source'. *Shakespeare Reproduced: The text in history and ideology*. Edited by Jean E. Howard and Marion F. O'Connor (London: Methuen, 1987). pp. 242–64.

2. Howard Felperin, *Shakespearean Representation: Mimesis and Modernity in Elizabethan Tragedy* (Princeton: Princeton University Press, 1977), p. 138.

3. Girard, p. 43–4.

4. Girard, p. 49.

5. Stephen Booth, *King Lear, Macbeth, Indefinition, and Tragedy* (New Haven: Yale University Press, 1983), p. 95.

6. Kiernan Ryan, p. 59.

7. Kenneth Muir urges the reader to 'Note the tailoring metaphor, of which there are many in the course of the play.' *Macbeth*, edited by Kenneth Muir. The Arden Shakespeare (London: Methuen, 1982), p. 7.

8. Goldberg, p. 249.

9. *Shakespeare and the Problem of Meaning*, p. 105.

10. *Ibid.*

11. Kierkegaard, *The Concept of Dread*, trans. Walter Lowrie (1944; rpt. Princeton: Princeton University Press, 1957) p. 40. Quoted by King-Kok Cheung, 'Shakespeare and Kierkegaard: 'Dread' in *Macbeth*', *Shakespeare Quarterly*, 35 (1984), p. 434.

12. See Geoffrey Bullough, *Narrative and Dramatic Sources of Shakespeare*, VII (London: Routledge Kegan Paul, 1973), pp. 431–432.
13. Jan Kott, *Shakespeare our Contemporary* (London: Methuen, 1966). p. 74.
14. Dennis Biggins, 'Sexuality, Witchcraft, and Violence in *Macbeth*', *Shakespeare Studies*, VII (1975), p. 265.
15. Biggins, pp. 255–75.
16. Biggins, 267.
17. *Angel With Horns*, p. 222.
18. Biggins argues that 'it is possible that Shakespeare's tailless rat is intended to suggest . . . sexual malignity in the succubus-incubus exchange of roles' (p. 262).

Index